MEMOIRS
FANSH

INTRODUCTION

There is a deathless charm, despite the efforts of modern novelists and playwrights to render it stale and hackneyed, attaching to the middle of the seventeenth century—that period of upheaval and turmoil which saw a stately debonnaire Court swept away by the flames of Civil War, and the reign of an usurper succeeded by the Restoration of a discredited and fallen dynasty.

So long as the world lasts, events such as the trial and execution of Charles Stuart will not cease to appeal to the imagination and touch the hearts of those at least who bring sentiment to bear on the reading of history.

It is not to the dry-as-dust historian, however, that we go for illuminating side-lights on this ever-fascinating time, but rather to the pen-portraits of Clarendon, the noble canvases of Van Dyck, and above all to the records of individual experience contained in personal memoirs. Of these none is more charmingly and vivaciously narrated or of greater historic value and interest than the following memoir (first published in 1830) of Sir Richard Fanshawe, "Knight and Baronet, one of the Masters of the Requests, Secretary of the Latin Tongue, Burgess of the University of Cambridge, and one of His Majesty's Most Honourable Privy Council of England and Ireland, and His Majesty's Ambassador to Portugal and Spain." It was written by his widow in the evening of her days, after a life of storm and stress and many romantic adventures at home and abroad, for the benefit of the only son who survived to manhood of fourteen children, most of whom died in their chrisom robes and whose baby bones were laid to rest in foreign churchyards.

Two contemporaries of Lady Fanshawe, Mrs. Hutchinson and the Duchess of Newcastle, also wrote lives of their husbands, which continue to live as classics in our literature. But the Royalist Ambassador's wife is incomparably more sparkling and anecdotic than the Puritan Colonel's, and she does not adopt the somewhat tiresome "doormat" attitude of wifely adoration towards the subject of her memoir which "Mad Margaret" (as Pepys called her Grace of Newcastle) thought fitting when she took up her fatally facile pen to endow her idolised lord with all the virtues and all the graces and every talent under the sun.

Yet with less lavishly laid on colours, how vivid is the portrait Lady Fanshawe has painted for posterity of the gallant gentleman and scholar, one of those "very perfect gentle knights" which that age produced; loyal and religious, with the straightforward simple piety that held unwaveringly to the Anglican Church in which he had been born and brought up.

And of herself, too, she unconsciously presents a series of charming pictures. The description of her girlhood is a glimpse into the bringing up of a Cavalier maiden of quality, of the kind that is invaluable in a reconstruction of the past from the domestic side. In the town-house in Hart Street which her father, Sir John Harrison, rented for the winter months from "my Lord Dingwall," where she was born, her education was carried on "with all the advantages the time afforded." She learnt French, singing to the lute, the virginals, and the art of needlework, and confesses that though she was quick at learning she was very wild and loved "riding, running and all active pastimes."

One can picture the light-hearted "hoyting girl" breaking loose when she found herself at Balls in Hertfordshire, where the family spent the summer, and skipping and jumping for sheer joy at being alive. And then we see her at fifteen suddenly sobered by the death of her mother, a lady of "excellent beauty and good understanding," and taking upon her young shoulders the entire management of her father's household. With naive satisfaction she tells of how well she succeeded and how she won the esteem of her mother's relations and friends, being ever "ambitious to keep the best company," which she thanks God she did all the days of her life.

Her father, like other loyal gentlemen, cheerfully suffered beggary in the King's cause. His estates and property were confiscated and he himself arrested. He managed to escape to Oxford, whither his daughters followed him, to lodge over a baker's shop in a poor garret with scarcely any clothes or money, they who had till then lived in "great plenty and great order."

The seat of learning was strangely transformed by the presence there of the moribund Court indulging in its last fling of gaieties and gallantries on the eve of the debacle of

Marston Moor. Soldiers swarmed in the streets and were billeted over the college gates, and gardens and groves were the trysting-place of courtiers and beautiful ladies in that fair spring-time. Oxford melted down its plate for the King and gave up its ancient halls to masques and plays for the amusement of the Queen.

Sir John Harrison and his young daughters played their part in this brilliant society. Mistress Anne's tender heart was moved to pity by the "sad spectacle of war," when starving, half-naked prisoners were marched past the windows of their lodging, but nothing could damp for long her high spirits and girlish gaiety. We are told (not by herself, but by the arch-gossip, old Aubrey) that in the company of Lady Isabella Thynne, brightest star of the Stuart Court, "fine Mistress Anne" played a practical joke on Dr. Kettle, the woman-hating President of Trinity, who resented the intrusion of petticoats into his garden, "dubbed Daphne by the wits." The lady in question aired herself there in a fantastic garment cut after the pattern of the angels, with her page and singing boy wafting perfumes and soft music before her, an apparition not likely to soothe the gigantic, choleric doctor. Lady Isabella and her friend Anne Harrison figure in one of the most graphic and remarkable chapters of "John Inglesant," in which the author has also drawn largely from these memoirs for a foundation to one of his imaginary episodes. The girl of eighteen, full of life and enthusiasm, was doubtless flattered at being taken up by the fashionable Court beauty, and may have allowed herself to be led into rather dangerous frolics, till Richard Fanshawe, a connection of her mother's family whom she had not met before, came to wait on the King at Christ Church. The two were thrown much together, and we may be sure Anne's time was now claimed by one she admired even more fervently than the eccentric Lady Isabella. Sir Richard wooed and won his fair young kinswoman amidst the alarums of war, and they were married at Wolvercot Church in May 1644, when the fritillaries were in bloom along the banks of Isis and Cavaliers still made merry in the last stronghold of a waning cause.

It must have been a picturesque group which assembled at the altar of the little quiet country church; the joyous bride with her fair young sister and handsome father of whom she was so proud, and the genial bridegroom who was of "more than the common height of men," and so popular that every one, even the King, called him Dick. Those troublous times had reduced the fortunes of both Harrisons and Fanshawes to the lowest ebb, and the young couple started their married life on 20 pounds and the forlorn hope of their Sovereign's promise of eventual compensation. When her husband went to Bristol with the Prince of Wales, we see the young wife left at Oxford, in delicate health, with scarcely a penny and a dying first-born. She relates how she was sitting in the garden of St. John's College breathing the air for the first time after her illness, when a letter came from Bristol, to her "unspeakable joy" containing fifty gold pieces and a summons to join Mr. Fanshawe, and how there was a sound of drums beating in the roadway under the garden wall, and she went up to the Mount to see Sir Charles Lee's company of soldiers march past, and as she stood leaning against a tree a volley of shot was fired to salute her, and she narrowly escaped being hit by a brace of bullets which struck the tree two inches above her head.

Thus began the long series of separations, reunions, hardships, and extraordinary adventures which this brave, fair Royalist passed through. Like Queen Henrietta Maria, she seems hardly ever to have gone to sea without being nearly "cast away." From Red Abbey in Ireland she and her babies and servants had to fly at the peril of their lives through "an unruly tumult with swords in their hands." On the Isles of Scilly she was put ashore more dead than alive, and plundered of all her possessions by the sailors. At Portsmouth she and her husband were fired upon by Dutch men-of-war, and another time they were shipwrecked in the Bay of Biscay. Yet her buoyant temperament was never crushed. She might have said with Shakespeare's Beatrice, "A star danced when I was born," so infinite was her capacity for keeping on the "windy side of care."

It was the old "hoyting girl" spirit still alive in her which prompted her to borrow the cabin boy's blue thrum-cap and tarred coat for half a crown to stand beside her husband on the deck when they were threatened by a Turkish galley on their way to Spain. But it was the true womanly spirit, tender, loving, devoted, which, after the Battle of Worcester, where Sir Richard was made a prisoner, took her every morning on foot when four boomed from the steeples, along the sleeping Strand to stand beneath his prison window on the bowling-green

2

at Whitehall. This happened during the wettest autumn that ever was known, and "the rain went in at her neck and out at her heels."

Sir Richard was released on parole by Cromwell, and for seven years the Fanshawes lived in comparative retirement in London and at Tankersley, the seat of the Lord Strafford in Yorkshire. Here they planted fruit-trees, and Sir Richard completed most of his literary work. Even when he was walking out of doors he was seen generally with some book in his hand, "which oftentimes was poetry." He translated the "Lusiad" of de Camoens, Guarini's famous pastoral the "Pastor Fido," and various pieces from Horace and Virgil. In Yorkshire their favourite little daughter Nan, the "dear companion of her mother's travels and sorrows," died of small-pox, and they left it for Hertfordshire, where the news of the Protector's death reached them in 1658.

They were allowed now to join the Court in France, and the exiled King appointed his faithful servant Dick Fanshawe Master of the Requests and Latin Secretary. He and his wife came home with the King at the Restoration, and her account of that gala voyage is one of the brightest and most vivid that has survived. It seems literally to burst with the jubilation and new hopes born by this event in a long- distracted country.

Charles II. gave Sir Richard his portrait framed in diamonds, and sent him first on an embassy to Portugal to negotiate his marriage, and then appointed him to the still more important post of Ambassador to Spain. On June 26, 1666, he died at Madrid of fever at the age of fifty-eight.

The England to which his wife brought his body had not fulfilled the high hopes and dreams of the Restoration. The vice, and laxity of morals into which it was sinking, would certainly have been repugnant to the clean-living, high-souled statesman, and we can hardly think him unhappy in the time of his death.

He was buried with much pomp in the Church of St. Mary at Ware, and his monument stands in a side chapel near the chancel. There, thirteen years later, his loyal lady and sprightly biographer was laid beside him in the vault and beneath the monument which she says: "Cost me two hundred pounds; and here if God pleases I intend to lie myself."

An unfinished sentence gives a pathetic close to these pages, so full of touches of humour, keen observation and racy anecdote. It would seem as if the hand which wielded so descriptive and ready a pen had wearied of its task; as if, at last, the sunny nature was overcast and the merry heart saddened. But surely not another word is needed to make the narrative more perfect. Those who first become acquainted with it in this reprint will meet with many things less familiar than Lady Fanshawe's moving account of her leave-taking from Charles I. at Hampton Court, which has been quoted hundreds of times. They will be thrilled by at least three stories of the supernatural told with the elan and consummate simplicity that exceeds art, and they will be charmed with the ingenuousness of the writer when she writes about herself, and her masterly little sketches by the way of such characters of the time as Sir Kenelm Digby and Lord Goring, son of the Earl of Norwich. Indeed, we venture to think they cannot fail to find the whole book delightful, because, though relating to a long-vanished past, it is as livingly human and fresh as if written yesterday.

BEATRICE MARSHALL.

NOTES ON THE ILLUSTRATIONS

As will be seen from the rough pedigree appended, the Baronetcy became extinct in 1694 with Sir Richard, Lady Fanshawe's son; while the Viscountcy, which was given to this Sir Richard's uncle, Thomas, came to an end in 1716 with Simon, the fifth Viscount. The knightly and lordly branches having failed, the tail male was represented by the Fanshawes of Jenkins, of Parsloes, and of Great Singleton.

The first branch became extinct in 1705, Sir Thomas Fanshawe of Jenkins leaving no male issue, and thus the heirlooms have descended to the two latter branches. The representatives of both these families possess the portraits, manuscripts, &c., many of which came originally from Ware Park,[Footnote: By the will of Sir Henry Fanshawe, who dies in 1616, it appears that some of the older pictures came from the "gallery," and his house in Warwick Lane. He directed they should be brought to Ware Park and remain as heirlooms.] the parental house of Lady Fanshawe's Royalist husband, as well as from Jenkins and Parsloes.

But before speaking of the heirlooms it may not be out of place to say something of these old seats of the Fanshawes and one or two other places mentioned in the Memoirs.

Parsloes, which stands partly in the parish of Barking and partly in Dagenham (Essex), is now in a very forlorn and dilapidated condition. Alterations that have been made from time to time, particularly the embellishments of 1814, which have somewhat given the old mansion a Strawberry-Hill-Gothic appearance, have in a measure destroyed its original character. Yet some panelled rooms remain, and some fine carved stone fireplaces that were removed here many years ago from the adjacent Elizabethan mansion, Eastbury House. [Footnote: Vide "Picturesque Old Houses."]

Jenkins, the more important estate, which passed away from the family in the early part of the eighteenth century, was a large square-moated timber house with two towers. Remains of the old fishponds and terraces may still be traced (about a mile from Parsloes), but nothing remains of the house or of a later structure which followed it. Indeed, the very name is now forgotten.

The mansion Ware Park has also long since been pulled down and rebuilt. It was sold owing to Sir Henry Fanshawe's losses in the Royalist cause.

Of the Derbyshire seat, Fanshawe Gate, at Holmesfield near Dronfield, there are still some picturesque remains, and the Church of Dronfield contains some good sixteenth-century brasses to the early members of the family.

Lady Fanshawe's parental house, Balls Park, near Hertford, though much modernised of recent years, dates back from the reign of Charles I. By intermarriage the estate passed to the Townshends, and the late Marquis sold it a few years ago.

Among the Townshend heirlooms which were dispersed in March 1904, were many portraits of the Harrisons, including a fine full-length of Lady Anne's Cavalier brother, William, who died fighting for the King in 1643.[Footnote: As the present owner of Balls Park, Sir G. Faudel- Phillips, was a conspicuous purchaser at this sale, it may be presumed some of the Harrison portraits have found their way back to their original home.]

"Little Grove," East Barnet, another place mentioned in the Memoirs, was rebuilt in 1719, and renamed "New Place."

It would be interesting if the position of Lady Fanshawe's lodgings in Chancery Lane, "at my cousin Young's," could be located. The house there that her husband rented from Sir George Carey in 1655-6, in all probability was the same which is mentioned in the artist George Vertue's MS. Collections as the old timber house that was once the dwelling of Cardinal Wolsey. In a "great room above stairs," he said, were carved arms and supporters of the Carews [Careys], who had repaired the ceilings, &c. At the time he wrote the building was used as a tavern. [Footnote: Vide Notes and Queries. Second Series, vol. xii., pp. 1, 81; also Middlesex and Hertfordshire Notes and Querie., vol. iii., p. 30.] The house on the north side of Lincoln's Inn Fields known as "The Pine Apples," where Lady Fanshawe was living at the time of her husband's death, has disappeared with the other old residences on that side of the square. Nothing is said in the Memoirs to locate the building where she met her husband when he was brought to London a prisoner after Worcester fight. The room in Whitehall facing the Bowling-green of course perished in the fire which destroyed the Palace at the end of the seventeenth century. [Footnote: A description of Borstal Tower mentioned in the Memoirs will be found in "Picturesque Old Houses."]

In regard to the monument of Sir Richard in Ware Church, which was erected to his memory by Lady Fanshawe, it is strange that there is no record of the interment in the Register. In the Register of All Saints Church, Hertford,[Footnote: The old church, including a fine monument to the Harrisons, was completely destroyed by fire a few years ago.] however, it is stated that the body was first interred in Sir John Harrison's vault:—"1671, May 18. Sir Richard Fanshawe, Ambassador, was taken out of this vault and laid in his vault at Ware." The monument was formerly in the Chapel at the south side of Ware Church, and was afterwards removed to the east wall of the south transept. No memorial marks the last resting-place of Lady Fanshawe. She was interred in the new vault that had been prepared for her husband under St. Mary's Chapel.

As before stated, the family portraits are now in the possession of the descendants of the half-brothers William [Footnote: It was William who married Mary Sarsfield, nee Walter,

4

the Duke of Monmouth's sister. Vide "King Monmouth."] and John Fanshawe, the sons of Lady Fanshawe's cousin, John Fanshawe.

The portraits of the Parsloes branch remained in the old Essex house until some thirty years ago, when they were removed to a town residence. They included Lady Fanshawe's portrait (reproduced here), the original of that engraved in her Memoirs in 1830 (by no means too faithfully); portraits of her husband Sir Richard, by Dobson [Footnote: An interesting portrait of Sir Richard in fancy dress by Dobson is at West Horsley Place.] and Lely; Sir Simon (the rake), with Naseby Field in the background: Sir Richard's grandfather, Thomas, Remembrancer to Queen Elizabeth; Alice, the second wife of Sir Richard's cousin, John of Parsloes (the daughter of his cousin Sir Thomas Fanshawe of Jenkins, and the mother-in-law of the Duke of Monmouth's half-sister, Mary Walter); Sir Richard's nephew, Thomas, the second Viscount (in breastplate and flowing wig), and his second wife, Lady Sarah, the daughter of Sir John Evelyn and widow of Sir John Wray. [Footnote: The ancient Lincolnshire family of Wray is mentioned in the Introduction of "King Monmouth" in connection with the remarkable portrait of the Duke after decapitation, which formerly was in the possession of Sir Cecil Wray. Since writing on this subject it occurs to me that it is very possible that the picture may have come originally to the Wrays through Lady Sarah Fanshawe, her husband being a cousin of the Duke's sister's second husband. Mary Fanshawe, nee Walter, it is very possible may have come into the possession of the portrait (perhaps after Henrietta, Lady Wentworth's death, for whom there is a tradition the picture was originally painted), and her straitened circumstances may have induced her to part with the work to the relatives of her kinswoman.]

The original MS. of the Memoirs (of which, thanks to the courtesy of the owner, Mr. E. J. Fanshawe, I am able to give an illustration) is bound in old red leather, and bears the Fanshawe arms. It was written in 1676 for Lady Fanshawe's "most dear and only" surviving son. This Sir Richard, the second Baronet, died in Clerkenwell in July 1694, having some years previously had the misfortune through illness to become deaf and dumb.

Comment at various times has been made upon the inaccuracy of the printed Memoirs, but judging from a personal inspection of the original, there appear to be but few serious errors. [Footnote: "Turning" for "Trimming instruments" (in Lady Anne's will), and such like slips. See p. 29.]

It must, however, be pointed out that the editor, Sir Harris Nicholas, only used a COPY of the Memoirs which was made from the original in 1766 by Charlotte Colman, Lady Fanshawe's great grand-daughter. The editor's transcript, though made ten years later, was not published until half a century afterwards. [Footnote: Vide Preface of 1830 Edition.] I draw attention to this fact as the Rev. T. L. Fanshawe, the grandfather of the present owner of the MS., was under the impression that his original Memoirs when lent to a friend had been copied and printed without permission, which in the face of the above statement could not have been the case. [Footnote: I have been indebted to Mr. Walter Crouch, Mr. R. T. Andrews, and to Mr. H. W. King's Notes on the Fanshawe Family, 1868-72, for some of the above information.]

ALLAN FEA.

CONTENTS

LIST OF ILLUSTRATIONS

INTRODUCTORY MEMOIR

It may, possibly, be thought unnecessary to prefix to this work a biographical sketch of the persons whose careers are faithfully related in it; and it may be considered an act of imprudence to place the cold and measured statements of an Editor in juxta-position with the nervous and glowing narrative of the amiable historian of the lives of her husband and herself. The latter objection, however true, ought not to prevent such remarks being made as may cause her labours to be better understood, and more highly appreciated; especially, as information can be supplied, and in a few instances, comments submitted, which may render that justice to the writer it was impossible for her to do to herself.

These pages will, however, contain a statement of the chief events of the lives of Sir Richard and Lady Fanshawe; and although most of them are mentioned in her Memoir, they are so frequently interrupted by anecdotes and reflections, as well as by accounts of places and ceremonies, that it is often difficult to follow her. This article may then be considered as the outline of a picture, which is filled up by a far abler and more pleasing artist; or, perhaps, it bears a nearer resemblance to the graphic references which generally accompany the descriptions of paintings, for the purpose of illustrating them.

The genealogy of the Fanshawe family is so fully stated in the Memoir, that it is not requisite to allude to the subject, farther than to observe, that Sir Richard was descended from an ancient and respectable house; that many of its members filled official situations under the Crown, and were honoured with Knighthood; that he was the fifth and youngest son of Sir Henry Fanshawe, of Ware Park, in Hertfordshire, Knight, by Elizabeth, daughter of Thomas Smythe, Esq., Farmer of the Customs to Queen Elizabeth, the younger son of an ancient Wiltshire family, and ancestor of the Viscounts Strangford; and that his eldest brother was raised to the peerage by the title of Viscount Fanshawe, of Dromore, in Ireland.

Sir Richard Fanshawe was born at Ware Park, in June 1608, and was baptized on the 12th of that month. His father having died in 1616, when he was little more than seven years old, the care of his education devolved upon his mother, who placed him under the celebrated schoolmaster, Thomas Farnaby; and in November 1623 he was admitted a Fellow-commoner of Jesus College, Cambridge, where he is said to have prosecuted his studies with success, and to have evinced a taste for classical literature. Being intended for the Bar, he was entered of the Inner Temple on the 22nd of January 1626; but that profession ill-accorded with his genius, and he appears to have selected it in obedience to the wishes of his mother, rather than from his own choice. It has been supposed that he continued his legal pursuits until her death left him free to follow his inclination to travel;

6

but this is not the fact, as he had returned to England before her decease. At what period he abandoned the law is not known; but about 1627 he went abroad, with the view of acquiring foreign languages. Lady Fanshawe says that the whole stock of money with which he commenced his travels did not exceed eighty-five pounds; that he proceeded first to Paris, where he remained for twelve months, and thence went to Madrid; and that he did not return to England for some years. In 1630 he was appointed Secretary to Lord Aston's embassy to the Court of Spain, in consequence of the information which he possessed of the country; but in attaining that knowledge he spent great part of his patrimony, which amounted only to 50 pounds per annum, and 1500 pounds in money.

When Lord Aston was recalled, Mr. Fanshawe remained as the Charge d'Affaires until Sir Arthur Hopton was nominated Ambassador to Madrid; and he arrived in England in 1637 or 1638. For two years after his return, he seems to have been in constant expectation of some appointment, but his views were frustrated by Secretary Windebank. At the expiration of that time, his eldest brother resigned to him the situation of Remembrancer of the Court of Exchequer, but upon terms which prevented its being of any immediate pecuniary advantage. The Civil War, however, then broke out and being one of the King's sworn servants, he attended his Majesty to Oxford, where he met the fair author of these Memoirs.

Anne, the eldest daughter of Sir John Harrison, of Balls, in the county of Hertford, by Margaret, daughter of Robert Fanshawe, of Fanshawe Gate Esq., great uncle of Sir Richard Fanshawe, was born in St. Olave's, Hart Street, London, on the 25th of March 1625. Of her education and early life she has given a pleasing description, and, until the Civil War, her family lived in uninterrupted happiness. Her father having warmly espoused the Royal cause, he attended the Court to Oxford, and desired his daughters to come to him in that city, where they endured many privations, "living in a baker's house in an obscure street, and sleeping in a bad bed in a garret, with bad provisions, no money, and little clothes." The picture of Oxford at that moment is truly deplorable, and the sufferings of the royalists appear to have been very severe, but which she describes as having been borne "with a martyr-like cheerfulness." The offer of a Baronetcy to her father—the only return which it was then in the power of the Crown to bestow, for the heavy losses he had sustained—was gratefully declined on the ground of poverty. In 1644 important changes took place in her family, or, as she poetically expresses it, alluding to the state of public affairs, "as the turbulence of the waves disperses the splinters of the rock," so were they separated. Her brother William died in consequence of a fall from his horse, which was shot under him in a skirmish against a party of the Earl of Essex the year before; and on the 18th of May she became the wife of Mr. Fanshawe, in Wolvercot Church, two miles from Oxford, being then in her twentieth year, and her husband about thirty-six. He was at that time Secretary at War, and was promised promotion the first opportunity. The fortune of each was in expectation: they were, she says, "truly merchant adventurers," their whole capital being only twenty pounds; and, to preserve the simile, that capital was laid out in the articles of his trade—in pens, ink, and paper. What was wanting in money was amply supplied by prudence and affection; and there is no difficulty in believing her assurance, that they lived better than those whose prospects were much brighter.

Whilst at Oxford, in 1644, the University conferred upon Mr. Fanshawe the degree of Doctor of Laws. In the beginning of March 1645 he attended the Prince to Bristol, but in consequence of his wife's confinement, she did not accompany him; and the circumstances of their separation are affecting. She joined him in that city in May, at which time he was appointed Secretary to the Prince of Wales, but in consequence of the plague they quitted Bristol, in July 1645, and proceeded with his Royal Highness to Barnstaple, and thence to Launceston and Truro, in Cornwall. From Truro the Court removed to Pendennis Castle; and early in April 1646 the Prince and his suite embarked for the Scilly Islands. Great as their privations were at Oxford, they were much exceeded by their sufferings at Scilly; and no one can peruse the description of their voyage to and lodgings in that island with indifference. To illness were added cold and hunger: they were plundered by their friends in flying from their enemies; and to add to the misery of their situation, Mrs. Fanshawe was very near her confinement.

7

After passing three weeks in that desolate place, the Prince and his suite went to Jersey, where they were hospitably received; and where Mrs. Fanshawe gave birth to her second child. On the Prince's quitting Jersey in July, for Paris, Mr. Fanshawe's employment ceased; and he remained in that island with Lord Capell, Lord Hopton, and the Chancellor, for a fortnight after his Royal Highness's departure, when he and his wife went to Caen, to his brother Lord Fanshawe, who was ill, leaving their infant at Jersey, under the care of Lady Carteret, the wife of the Governor. From Caen, Mrs. Fanshawe was sent to England, by her husband, to raise money: she arrived in London early in September 1646, where she succeeded in obtaining permission for him to compound for his estates for the sum of 300 pounds, and to return.

They continued in England until October 1647, living in great seclusion; and in July in that year, whilst the unfortunate Charles was at Hampton Court, Mr. Fanshawe waited upon him, and received his instructions to proceed to Madrid. Mrs. Fanshawe states that she had three audiences of his Majesty at Hampton Court, and her description of the last interview with which she and her husband were honoured, exhibits the injured monarch as a husband, a father, a master, a sovereign, and a Christian, in the most pleasing light, and is ample evidence of the natural goodness of his heart. "The last time I ever saw him," she says, "was on taking my leave. I could not refrain from weeping, and when he saluted me, I prayed to God to preserve his Majesty with long life and happy years. He stroked me on the cheek, and said, 'Child, if God pleaseth it shall be so; but both you and I must submit to God's will, and you know in what hands I am.' Turning to Mr. Fanshawe, he said, 'Be sure, Dick, [Footnote: That the Royal family were accustomed to address Mr. Fanshawe in so familiar a manner, appears from a letter from the Duke of York, afterwards James the Second, dated at Paris, 18th November, 1651, to Sir Edward Nicholas: "I have received yours of the 8th of November from the Hague, and with it that from DICK FANSHAWE."—Evelyn's Correspondence, vol. v. p. 188.] to tell my son all that I have said, and deliver those letters to my wife. Pray God bless her! I hope I shall do well;' and taking him in his arms, observed, 'Thou hast ever been an honest man, and I hope God will bless thee, and make thee a happy servant to my son, whom I have charged in my letter to continue his love and trust to you;' adding, 'I do promise you, that if ever I am restored to my dignity, I will bountifully reward you both for your services and sufferings.'"

In the few days they passed at Portsmouth, previous to their quitting England in October 1647, they narrowly escaped being killed by a shot fired into the town by the Dutch fleet. From that place they embarked for France, but returned to England, in April 1648, by Jersey, whence they brought with them their daughter, whom they had left under the care of Lady Carteret. In September Mr. Fanshawe attended the Prince of Wales on board the fleet in the Downs, in which a division existed, part being for the King and part for the Parliament. The Prince resolved to reduce the latter to obedience by force, but a storm separated the ships, and prevented an engagement. Three months afterwards, Mr. Fanshawe went to Paris on the Prince's affairs, whither he was followed by his wife; and they passed six weeks there in the society of the Queen-Mother and the Princess Royal and their suite, amongst whom was the poet Waller and his wife. From Paris they went to Calais, where they met Sir Kenelm Digby, who related some of his extraordinary stories: from that town she again went to England with the hope of raising money for her husband's subsistence abroad and her own at home. Mr. Fanshawe was sent to Flanders; and thence, in the February following, into Ireland, to receive whatever money Prince Rupert could raise by the fleet under his command, but that effort proved unsuccessful. At her husband's desire, Mrs. Fanshawe proceeded with her family to join him, and landed at Youghal after a hazardous voyage. They took up their residence at Red Abbey, a house belonging to Dean Boyle, near Cork, and passed six months in comparative tranquillity, receiving great kindness from the nobility and gentry of the neighbourhood.

Their happiness, however, was but transitory. On the 2nd of September in that year Mr. Fanshawe was created a Baronet; and it is singular that no other allusion should occur to the circumstance in the Memoir than a notice of his having left the patent in Scotland before the battle of Worcester.

The Queen received them at Paris with great attention; and after many acts of favour, she despatched Sir Richard to the King, who was then on his way to Scotland. Lady Fanshawe and her husband proceeded to Calais, it being necessary that she should go to England to procure money for his journey, and in the mean time he intended to reside in Holland; but circumstances caused him to be immediately sent into Scotland, where he was received with marked kindness by the King and by the York party, who gave him the custody of the Great Seal and Privy Signet. No persuasions could induce him to take the Covenant; but he performed the duties of his office with a zeal and temper which, we are told, obtained for him the esteem of all parties.

Lady Fanshawe continued in London, in a state of great uneasiness about Sir Richard, having two young children to maintain, with very limited resources; and to add to her discomfort, she was again very near her confinement. She observes, that she seldom went out of her lodgings, and spent her time chiefly in prayer for the deliverance of the King and her husband. A daughter, Elizabeth, was born on the 24th of June, and on her recovery she went to her brother-in-law's, at Ware Park, where the news reached her of the battle of Worcester, on the 3rd of September; and after some days' suspense, she learned that Sir Richard was taken prisoner.

She then hastened to town, intending to seek him wherever he might be; but on her arrival she learned from him that he would shortly be brought to London, and he appointed a place near Charing Cross where she should meet him. Their interview lasted only a few hours; after which he was conveyed to Whitehall, and was closely confined there for ten weeks, expecting daily to be put to death. The manner in which she went secretly to his prison at four o'clock every morning, and her unwearied zeal to alleviate his sufferings, afford a beautiful example of female devotion; and it was owing to her exertions alone that he was ultimately released on bail.

Illness induced Sir Richard to go to Bath, in August 1652, the greater part of the winter of which year they passed at Benford, in Hertfordshire; but having occasion to wait on the Earl of Strafford, in Yorkshire, his Lordship offered him a house in Tankersley Park, which he accepted. His family removed thither in March 1652, and during his residence there he amused himself in literary pursuits, and translated Luis de Camoens. The death of their favourite daughter Anne, on the 23rd of July 1654, at the age of between nine and ten, made them quit Tankersley, and they proceeded to Homerton, in Huntingdonshire, the seat of Sir Richard Fanshawe's sister, Lady Bedell, where they resided six months; when he being sent for to London, and forbidden to go beyond five miles of it, his wife and children removed to the metropolis. Excepting a visit to Frog Pool, in Kent, the residence of Sir Philip Warwick, they remained in London until July 1656, during which time Lady Fanshawe had two children, and her husband suffered severely from illness.

Tired of living in town, Sir Richard obtained permission to go to Bengy, in Hertfordshire, where he and his wife were attacked with an ague, which confined her to her bed for many months, and did not finally leave her for nearly two years, when a visit to Bath perfectly restored them both. The news of Cromwell's death, in September 1658, which reached them whilst in that city, caused them to go to London, with the hope of Sir Richard's getting released from his bail; and under the pretence of becoming tutor to the son of the Earl of Pembroke, whilst on his travels, he was permitted to leave England. On his arrival at Paris, he wrote to Lord Clarendon, acquainting him with his escape, and desiring him to inform his Majesty of the circumstance. About April 1659, his Lordship replied that the King was then going into Spain, but that on his return, which would be in the beginning of the winter, he should come to his Majesty, who in the meantime gave him the situations of one of the Masters of Requests, and Latin Secretary.

Sir Richard Fanshawe then requested his wife to come to Paris with part of his children, but her application for a passport was refused; and she relates the ingenious manner in which she imposed upon the Government, by obtaining a pass in the name of Anne Harrison; the pretended wife of a young merchant, and altering the word to Fanshawe, by which means she escaped to Calais, and joined her husband at Paris.

Charles the Second came to Combes, near Paris, on a visit to his mother, in November 1659, where Sir Richard and Lady Fanshawe had an interview with him, and were received most graciously, with promises of future protection. Sir Richard being desired to follow his Majesty to Flanders, he went thither in December, having previously sent his wife to London for money, where she arrived with her children in January 1660. Soon afterwards she followed him to Newport, Bruges, Ghent, and Brussels, where the Royal family of England were residing, by all of whom they were treated with kindness. After staying three weeks at Brussels, Sir Richard and Lady Fanshawe went to Breda, where they heard of the Restoration, at which place, in April, his Majesty is said to have conferred on him the honour of Knighthood, [Footnote: Biographia Britannica.] though the fact is not mentioned in the Memoir.

On joining the King at the Hague, he promised to reward Sir Richard's fidelity and sufferings, by appointing him Secretary of State; but through the machinations of "that false man," as Lady Fanshawe calls Lord Clarendon, the royal word was not fulfilled. When his Majesty embarked for England, Sir Richard was ordered to attend him in his own ship; and a frigate was appointed to convey his family. The morning after Charles's arrival at Whitehall, Lady Fanshawe, with some other ladies, waited upon him to offer their congratulations, on which occasion he assured her of his favour, and presented Sir Richard with his portrait set in diamonds. To the Parliament summoned immediately after the restoration he was returned for the University of Cambridge; and "had the good fortune," his affectionate biographer says, "to be the first chosen, and the first returned member of the Commons House in Parliament, after the King came home; and this cost him no more than a letter of thanks, and two brace of bucks, and twenty broad pieces of gold to buy them wine." To the jealousy of Lord Clarendon, who was anxious to remove Sir Richard from about the King's person, Lady Fanshawe imputes the circumstance of his being sent to Portugal to negotiate the marriage with the Princess Katharine, to whom he was charged to present his Majesty's picture; but this appointment is strong proof of the confidence which was reposed in his discretion and abilities. He returned to England in December, and during his absence Lady Fanshawe remained in London, where she gave birth to a daughter in January 1662. On the arrival of the Queen at Portsmouth, Sir Richard Fanshawe was sent to receive her, and was present at her marriage, the description of which ceremony is historically valuable.

Early in 1662 he was nominated a Privy Counsellor of Ireland: in August he was again sent on an embassy to Lisbon, and was accompanied by his wife and children. Their journey to Plymouth, their voyage, their arrival at Lisbon, their reception at Court, and the city, are minutely described. After a year's residence in Portugal, Sir Richard was recalled: he returned to London in September 1663, and proceeded to wait on the King at Bath, who was pleased to raise him to the rank of a Privy Counsellor. In January 1664, he was appointed Ambassador to the Court of Madrid, and having embarked at Portsmouth, with a numerous retinue, on board a squadron on the 31st of that month, they arrived at Cadiz on the 23rd of February.

Nearly the whole of the remainder of the Memoir is filled with an account of their journey to Madrid, of their splendid reception, of the manners of the Spaniards, of various places, and of public events and ceremonies. These descriptions display considerable judgment and quickness of observation, and contain some valuable information. Many of the anecdotes which occur are interesting, and like every other part of the narrative, they are told with a simplicity which renders it impossible to doubt their accuracy.

At Madrid, Lady Fanshawe gave birth to her son Richard; and the prayer which she breathes for his prosperity exhibits her piety and affection in lively colours. Sir Richard Fanshawe went on a mission to Lisbon in January 1664, and returned to Madrid early in March following. On the 17th of December 1665, he signed a treaty with the Spanish minister, but the King refused to ratify it, and he was recalled, when the Earl of Sandwich was sent to replace him, who arrived at Corunna in March following. Previous to this circumstance, Lady Fanshawe intended to return to England to see her father, who was on the verge of the grave; but she then resolved to wait for Sir Richard's departure.

She was now, however, destined to experience the severest of all her trials, in the death of her husband, who, after introducing Lord Sandwich at Court on the 15th of June, was seized with an ague, and expired on the 26th of the same month. [Footnote: According to the inscription on his monument, he died on the SIXTEENTH of June; the discrepancy arose from the difference in the style.]

No other language could convey an adequate idea of Lady Fanshawe's feelings under her loss, than that in which she has expressed them; and her address to the Almighty on her sufferings merits every possible praise.

Some of Sir Richard Fanshawe's biographers have imputed his death to a broken heart, in consequence of his being recalled; but this is a gratuitous assertion, for nothing of the kind is hinted in the Memoir, though the conduct of Lord Clarendon and others towards him is severely commented upon. His letter to the King on the occasion is preserved, from which it is evident that he felt his recall deeply, but the gracious communication by which it was accompanied lessened the severity of the act, and he seems anxiously to have looked forward to his arrival in England to defend his conduct.

Lady Fanshawe resolved on accompanying her husband's corpse to England; but, previous to her quitting Madrid, the Queen-Regent of Spain offered her a pension, and promised to provide for her children, if she and they would embrace the Roman Catholic faith; an offer, which it would be an insult to her memory to attribute any merit to her for refusing. Having disposed of her plate, furniture, and horses, she left the Siete Chimeneas, in a private manner, on the 8th of July, and observes, "Never did any ambassador's family come into Spain so gloriously, or went out so sad." She reached Bilboa on the 21st of July, where Sir Richard's corpse awaited her arrival, and remained there until the 3rd of October. The mournful train then proceeded towards England, by Bayonne and Paris, where they arrived on the 30th of October. After an audience of the Queen-Mother, Lady Fanshawe set out for Calais; and on the 2nd of November was conveyed to the Tower Wharf in a French vessel-of-war. On the 26th, the body of Sir Richard, attended by seven of the gentlemen of his suite, was interred in Allhallows Church, in Hertford, whence it was removed, in May 1671, to a vault in St. Mary's Chapel in Ware Church, where his widow erected a handsome monument, with the following inscription to his memory:—

P.M.S.

In Hypogeo, juxta hoc monumentum, jacet corpus nobilissimi viri RICARDI FANSHAWE, Equitis Aurati et Baronetti, ex antiqua illa familia de Ware Parke, in comitatu Hertfordiae, Henrici Fanshawe, Equitis Aurati, prolis decimae. Uxorem duxit Annam filiam natu maximam Johannis Harrison, Equitis Aurati, de Balls, in com. Hertfordiae; et ex ea suscepit sex filios et octo filias; e quibus supersunt Ricardus, Catherina, Margarita, Anna, et Elizabetha. Vir comitate morum, luce fidei, constantia, praestantissimus, qui olim (laetus exul) serenissimi regis Caroli Secundi calamitates fortiter amplexus est, in Rebus bellicis, ab eodem constitutus Secretarius, posteaque (Regno ei feliciter restaurato) libellorum supplicum Magister, a Latinis epistolis, a sanctioribus Regis consiliis tum Angliae, tum Hiberniae factus; pro Academia Cantabrigiensi Burgensis; Necnon ejusdem serenissimi Regis ad utrasque Aulas Portugal. et Hispan. Legatus, in quarum proxima, cum pulcherrimo officio suo functus esset, splendidissimam quamdiu egerat Vitam cum luctuosa morte commutavit. Monumentum hoc, cum Hypogeo, moestissima conjux pie posuit, quas etiam corpus Mariti sui ab urbe Madrid huc per terras transtulit.

Obiit 16 de Junii, anno Dom MDCLXVI aetatis suae LIX. [Footnote: Clutterbuck's History of Hertfordshire, vol. iii. page 311. The following arms occur on the monument: Quarterly, 1st and 4th, Or, a chevron between three fleurs-de-lis Sable, Fanshawe ancient; 2nd and 3rd, cheeky Argent and Azure, a cross Gules, Fanshawe modern, being an honourable augmentation granted in 1650: on an escutcheon in the centre, the arms of Ulster. Impaling, Cheeky, a cross, thereon five pheons' heads, pointing upwards. Harrison. Crest, on a wreath, Or and Azure, a dragon's head erased Or, vomiting fire. On a label under the arms these mottos: "Dux vitae ratio." "In Christo victoria."]

Sir Richard Fanshawe was buried with much pomp, and a full account of the ceremony occurs in his funeral certificate in the College of Arms.

From the King, the Queen, the Court, and some of the ministers, Lady Fanshawe received much sympathy and kindness; but, in common with every other person who had pecuniary claims on the Government, she experienced great difficulty in procuring the arrears due to her husband, and it was not until nearly three years that the whole was paid;

by which delay, she says, she sustained a loss of above two thousand pounds. At the instigation of Lord Shaftesbury, of whom she speaks with the utmost bitterness, she was obliged to pay the same amount for the plate furnished to the embassy.

Of the tardy manner in which Sir Richard Fanshawe's allowance was paid, and the embarrassment into which he was consequently thrown, he has left ample proof in his letter to his brother-in-law Sir Philip Warwick, dated a few weeks before his death; in which he tells him that he had been obliged to pawn his plate for his subsistence.

Lady Fanshawe states in a very feeling manner the situation in which she found herself after her husband's death; and it is scarcely possible to read her allusions to his long and faithful services, and the heavy sacrifices which he made, without admitting the justice of the charge so often brought against Charles, of being neglectful of his servants. It is, however, more than possible that the fault was not the monarch's alone. He was surrounded by greedy and selfish courtiers, each eager to advance his own interest, and possessed of similar claims on the ground of services; and as the spoils out of which they sought to enrich themselves were limited, it was an obvious point of policy to oppose the demands of others. The few years which succeeded the Restoration are among the most disgraceful in the annals of this country; and to the evidence which exists of the want of principle which characterised the Court of Charles the Second, these Memoirs are no slight addition. The monarch was heartless and profligate; his ministers, with very few exceptions, were intent alone on the promotion of their own interests; and services and sufferings were nothing in the balance against the influence of the royal mistresses. In such a state of things, merit availed but little; and with a host of other zealous adherents of the royal family, at a time when fidelity was attended with the fearful penalties attached to high treason, Sir Richard Fanshawe, after thirty years' devotion to his master, and spending a fortune in his cause, was sacrificed to the intrigues of his enemies, and probably was only spared by death from greater mortifications.

To this outline of the lives of Sir Richard and Lady Fanshawe little remains to be added. The Memoir, though continued to the year 1670, contains very few facts after her return to England which are deserving of notice. It is manifest that her hopes were destroyed, and that her only happiness consisted in reflecting on the past. Her first object was to reduce her establishment according to her altered fortune, and the second to educate her family. In 1670 she lost her excellent father, whose death added heavily to her misfortunes; but she possessed that resource against human woes which can only be inspired by a reliance upon Him who never deserts the widow and the fatherless. Her life had been marked by extreme vicissitudes; and at its conclusion—dark and cheerless as it was—she wisely looked for consolation where she had so frequently found it, and where, it may be confidently said, it is never sought in vain.

Of the conduct of Sir Richard Fanshawe, as a servant of the Crown, and as a husband and a father, sufficient is said in the Memoir; but it is desirable to notice his literary labours, which are stated in the Biographia Britannica to consist of—

1. An English translation, in rhyme, of the celebrated Italian pastoral, called "Il Pastor Fido, or, the Faithful Shepherd," written originally by Battista Guarini. Printed at London, 1646, 4to, and in 1664, 8vo.

2. Select parts of Horace translated into English, 1652, 8vo.

3. A translation from English into Latin verse, of "The Faithful Shepherdess," a pastoral, written originally by John Fletcher. London, 1658.

4. In the octavo edition of "The Faithful Shepherdess," anno 1664, are inserted the following poems by Sir Richard, viz.: 1. An Ode upon occasion of his Majesty's Proclamation in 1630, commanding the gentry to reside upon their estates in the country. 2. A summary Discourse on the Civil Wars of Rome, extracted from the best Latin writers in verse and prose. 3. An English translation of the fourth book of the Æneid of Virgil or the Loves of Dido and Æneas. 4. Two Odes out of Horace, relating to the civil wars of Rome, against covetous rich men. 5. He translated, from Portuguese, into English, "The Luciad, or Portugal's Historical Poem"; written originally by Luis de Camoens. London, 1655, fol. From the many corrections in the Translator's copy, in the possession of the late Edm. Turnor, Esq., it appears to have been very negligently printed, which may in some degree account for the remarks of Mr. Mickle on Sir Richard's translation. After his decease, namely in 1671,

two of his posthumous pieces in 4to were published, Querer per solo querer: "To love only for love's sake," a dramatic piece, represented before the King and Queen of Spain; and Fiestas de Aranjuez: "Festivals at Aranjuez"; both written originally in Spanish, by Antonio de Mendoza; upon occasion of celebrating the birthday of King Philip IV. in 1621, at Aranjuez. They were translated by Sir Richard in 1654, during his confinement at Tankersley Park, in Yorkshire; which situation induced him to write the following stanzas:

"Time was, when I, a pilgrim of the seas,
When I, 'midst noise of camps and court's disease,
Purloin'd some hours, to charm rude cares with verse,
Which flame of faithful shepherd did rehearse.
"But now, restrain'd from sea, from camp, from court,
And by a tempest blown into a port,
I raise my thoughts to muse of higher things,
And echo arms and loves of queens and kings.
"Which queens (despising crowns and Hymen's band)
Would neither man obey, nor man command;
Great pleasure from rough seas to see the shore;
Or, from firm land, to see the billows roar."

Sir Richard, to whom Mr. Campbell assigns the merit of having given "to our language some of its earliest and most important translations from modern literature," [Footnote: Specimens of the Poets.] wrote several other articles, which he had not leisure to complete; and it is said that "some of the before mentioned printed pieces have not all the perfection which our ingenious author could have given them, but that is not the case with his excellent translation of Pastor Fido." [Footnote: Biographia Britannica.]

That translation is highly complimented by Denham, who observes,

"Such is our pride, or folly, or our fate,
That few but such as cannot write translate;"
and after censuring servile translators, he says—
"Secure of fame, thou justly dost esteem
Less honour to create than to redeem;
That servile path thou nobly dost decline,
Of tracing word by word, and line by line."
And,
"That master's hand, which to the life can trace
The air, the line, the features, of the face,
May with a free and bolder stroke express
A varied posture, or a flatt'ring dress;
He could have made those like, who made the rest,
But that he knew his own design was best."

Part of Sir Richard Fanshawe's official correspondence, during his embassies in Spain and Portugal, was published in 1701, from which many extracts have been printed at the end of this volume; but the latest letter therein is dated 26th January 1665. The rough copies of his correspondence from that time until his death, are preserved in the Harleian MS. 7010, in the British Museum, the most interesting parts of which are added to the other extracts.

Lady Fanshawe wrote her Memoir in the year 1676, and died on the 20th January 1679-80, in her fifty-fifth year. Her will is dated on the 30th October, 31st Car. II., 1679, in which she desired that her body might be privately buried in the Chapel of St. Mary in Ware Church, close to her husband, in the vault which she had purchased of the Bishop of London. She ordered her house in Little Grove, in East Barnet, with all the jewels, plate, and pictures therein, to be sold. To her son, Sir Richard Fanshawe, she bequeathed the lease of the manor of Faunton Hall, in Essex, which she held of the Bishop of London, on condition that when he possessed his office in the Custom- House, or any other employment of the value of 500 pounds a year, he should pay to his eldest sister Katherine 1200 pounds, or deliver up the said lease to her. She also left him her own and her husband's picture set in gold, his father's picture by Lilly, and her own by Toniars, with all her seals, particularly a

13

gold ring, with an onyx-stone, engraved, her purse of medals, all the gold she had by her at the time of her death, a Spanish towel, and comeing-cloth, together with all the books, MSS., writings, &c., sticks, guns, swords, and turning instruments, which belonged to her late husband. To her daughter, Katherine Fanshawe, she left 600 pounds of which sum 500 pounds were given her by her grandfather, Sir John Harrison, at his decease, a warrant for a Baronet, probably her husband's, and all her jewels. To her daughters Anne Fanshawe and Elizabeth Fanshawe 600 pounds each, of which sums 500 pounds were given to each of them by their said grandfather. To her daughter Katherine she bequeathed the Work written by herself, by her said daughter Katherine, or by her sisters. She requested that her son Richard and her three daughters would wear mourning for three years after her decease, namely, mourning with plain linen, excepting either of them married in the meantime; and she appointed her eldest daughter, Katherine, her sole executrix, who proved her will on the 6th February 1679-80.

Of her numerous children, the following particulars have been gleaned from her Memoir and other sources.

1. HARRISON, born in the parish of St. John's Oxford, 22nd February 1644-5, and was there buried in the same year.

2. HENRY, born in Portugal Row, Lincoln's Inn Fields, London, 30th July 1647, died on the 20th October 1650, and was buried in the Protestant burying-ground at Paris.

3. RICHARD, born 8th June 1648, died before October 1650.

4. HENRY, born in November 1657, and dying in the same year, was buried in Bengy Church, in Hertfordshire.

5. RICHARD, born at Lisbon, 26th June 1663; he lived a few hours only, and was there buried in the Esperanza.

6. RICHARD, born at Madrid, 6th August 1665, to whom the Memoir was addressed. He succeeded his father in 1666, and became the second Baronet. He is said to have been deprived of his hearing, and at length of his speech, in consequence of a fever, and to have died unmarried about 1695, [Footnote: Le Neve's MSS. in the College of Arms.] when the Baronetcy became extinct.

The daughters were:

1. ANNE, born at Jersey, 7th June 1646; died at Tankersley Park, in Yorkshire, 20th July 1654, and was buried in the Parish Church of Tankersley.

2. ELIZABETH, born at Madrid, 13th July 1649; died a few days afterwards, and was buried in the Chapel of the French Hospital at Madrid.

3. ELIZABETH, born 24th June 1650; died at Foot's Cray, in Kent, in July 1656, and was there buried.

4. KATHERINE, born 30th July 1652, and was living, and unmarried, in May 1705.

5. MARGARET, born at Tankersley Park, in Yorkshire, 8th October 1653, married, before 1676, Vincent Grantham, of Goltho, in Lincolnshire, Esq. It is remarkable that she is not mentioned in her mother's will. She was living, and the wife or widow of Mr. Grantham, in May 1705.

6. ANN, born at Frog Pool, in Kent, 22nd February 1654-5, unmarried October 1679; but afterwards married —— Ryder, by whom she had a daughter, Ann Lawrence, who, with her mother, were living in May 1705.

7. MARY, born in London, 12th July 1656; died in August 1660, and was buried in All Saints' Church, Hertford.

8. ELIZABETH, born 22nd February 1662, to whom her mother bequeathed 600 pounds in her will in 1679, after which year nothing more of her has been found.

Although some trouble has been taken to trace the descendants of Sir Richard and Lady Fanshawe, all which has been discovered is, that their daughters became their co-heirs about 1695; that Sir Edmund Turnor, the husband of Lady Fanshawe's sister, in his will, dated 15th May 1705, and proved in 1708, mentions his nieces Fanshawe, Grantham, and niece Ann Fanshawe, alias Ryder, and Anne Lawrence, daughter of his niece Ryder; and that the MS. from which this volume is printed is said to have been transcribed in 1766 by Lady Fanshawe's "great granddaughter, Charlotte Colman."

MEMOIRS OF LADY FANSHAWE

I have thought it good to discourse to you, my most dear and only son, the most remarkable actions and accidents of your family, as well as those more eminent ones of your father; and my life and necessity, not delight or revenge, hath made me insert some passages which will reflect on their owners, as the praises of others will be but just, which is my intent in this narrative. I would not have you be a stranger to it; because, by the example, you may imitate what is applicable to your condition in the world, and endeavour to avoid those misfortunes we have passed through, if God pleases.

Endeavour to be innocent as a dove, but as wise as a serpent; and let this lesson direct you most in the greatest extremes of fortune. Hate idleness, and curb all passions; be true in all words and actions; unnecessarily deliver not your opinion; but when you do, let it be just, well-considered, and plain. Be charitable in all thought, word and deed, and ever ready to forgive injuries done to yourself, and be more pleased to do good than to receive good.

Be civil and obliging to all, dutiful where God and nature command you; but friend to one, and that friendship keep sacred, as the greatest tie upon earth, and be sure to ground it upon virtue; for no other is either happy or lasting.

Endeavour always to be content in that estate of life which it hath pleased God to call you to, and think it a great fault not to employ your time, either for the good of your soul, or improvement of your understanding, health, or estate; and as these are the most pleasant pastimes, so it will make you a cheerful old age, which is as necessary for you to design, as to make provision to support the infirmities which decay of strength brings: and it was never seen that a vicious youth terminated in a contented, cheerful old age, but perished out of countenance. Ever keep the best qualified persons company, out of whom you will find advantage, and reserve some hours daily to examine yourself and fortune; for if you embark yourself in perpetual conversation or recreation, you will certainly shipwreck your mind and fortune. Remember the proverb—such as his company is, such is the man, and have glorious actions before your eyes, and think what shall be your portion in Heaven, as well as what you desire on earth.

Manage your fortune prudently, and forget not that you must give God an account hereafter, and upon all occasions.

Remember your father, whose true image, though I can never draw to the life, unless God will grant me that blessing in you; yet, because you were but ten months and ten days old when God took him out of this world, I will, for your advantage, show you him with all truth, and without partiality.

He was of the highest size of men, strong, and of the best proportion; his complexion sanguine, his skin exceedingly fair, his hair dark brown and very curling, but not very long; his eyes grey and penetrating, his nose high, his countenance gracious and wise, his motion good, his speech clear and distinct. He never used exercise but walking, and that generally with some book in his hand, which oftentimes was poetry, in which he spent his idle hours; sometimes he would ride out to take the air, but his most delight was, to go only with me in a coach some miles, and there discourse of those things which then most pleased him, of what nature soever.

He was very obliging to all, and forward to serve his master, his country, and friend; cheerful in his conversation; his discourse ever pleasant, mixed with the sayings of wise men, and their histories repeated as occasion offered, yet so reserved that he never showed the thought of his heart, in its greatest sense, but to myself only; and this I thank God with all my soul for, that he never discovered his trouble to me, but went from me with perfect cheerfulness and content; nor revealed he his joys and hopes but would say, that they were doubled by putting them in my breast. I never heard him hold a disputation in my life, but often he would speak against it, saying it was an uncharitable custom, which never turned to the advantage of either party. He would never be drawn to the fashion of any party, saying he found it sufficient honestly to perform that employment he was in: he loved and used cheerfulness in all his actions, and professed his religion in his life and conversation. He was a true Protestant of the Church of England, so born, so brought up, and so died; his conversation was so honest that I never heard him speak a word in my life that tended to God's dishonour, or encouragement of any kind of debauchery or sin. He was ever much

15

esteemed by his two masters, Charles the First and Charles the Second, both for great parts and honesty, as for his conversation, in which they took great delight, he being so free from passion, that made him beloved of all that knew him, nor did I ever see him moved but with his master's concerns, in which he would hotly pursue his interest through the greatest difficulties.

He was the tenderest father imaginable, the carefullest and most generous master I ever knew; he loved hospitality, and would often say, it was wholly essential for the constitution of England: he loved and kept order with the greatest decency possible; and though he would say I managed his domestics wholly, yet I ever governed them and myself by his commands; in the managing of which, I thank God, I found his approbation and content.

Now you will expect that I should say something that may remain of us jointly, which I will do though it makes my eyes gush out with tears, and cuts me to the soul to remember, and in part express the joys I was blessed with in him. Glory be to God, we never had but one mind throughout our lives. Our souls were wrapped up in each other's; our aims and designs one, our loves one, and our resentments one. We so studied one the other, that we knew each other's mind by our looks. Whatever was real happiness, God gave it me in him; but to commend my better half, which I want sufficient expression for, methinks is to commend myself, and so may bear a censure; but, might it be permitted, I could dwell eternally on his praise most justly; but thus without offence I do, and so you may imitate him in his patience, his prudence, his chastity, his charity, his generosity, his perfect resignation to God's will, and praise God for him as long as you live here, and with him hereafter in the Kingdom of Heaven. Amen.

Your father was born in Ware Park, in the month of June, in the year of our Lord 1608, and was the tenth child of Sir Henry Fanshawe, whose father bought Ten, in Essex, and Ware Park, in Hertfordshire. This, your great-grandfather, came out of Derbyshire from a small estate, Fanshawe-Gate, being the principal part that then this family had, which exceeded not above two hundred pounds a year, and about so much more they had in the town and parish of Dronfield, within two miles of Fanshawe-Gate, where the family had been some hundreds of years, as appears by the church of Dronfield, in the chancel of which church I have seen several grave-stones with the names of that family, many of them very ancient; and the chancel, which is very old, was and is kept wholly for a burying-place for that family.

There is in the town a free school, with a very good house and noble endowment, founded by your great-grandfather, who was sent for to London in Henry the Eighth's time, by an uncle of his, and of his own name, to be brought up a clerk under his uncle Thomas Fanshawe, who procured your great-grandfather's life to be put with his in the patent of Remembrancers of his Majesty's Exchequer, which place he enjoyed after the death of his uncle, he having left no male issue, only two daughters, who had both great fortunes in land and money, and married into the best families in Essex in that time. This was the rise of your great-grandfather, who, with his office and his Derbyshire estate, raised the family to what it hath been and now is. He had one only brother, Robert Fanshawe, who had a good estate in Derbyshire, and lived in Fanshawe-Gate, which he hired of his eldest brother, your great-grandfather.

In this house my mother was born, Margaret, the eldest daughter of Robert, your great-great-uncle: he married one of the daughters of Rowland Eyes, of Bradway, in the same county of Derby, by whom he had twelve sons and two daughters: that family remains in Dronfield to this day.

Your great-grandfather married Alice Bourchier, of the last Earl of Bath's family,[Footnote: This was not the fact. She was the daughter of Anthony Bourchier, Esq., of the County of Gloucester, a family in no way connected with the noble house of Bath.] by whom he had only one son that lived, Henry, which was your grandfather; afterwards, when he had been two years a widower, he married one of the daughters of Customer Smythe, who had six sons and six daughters: his sons were Sir John Smythe, Sir Thomas Smythe, Sir Richard Smythe, Sir Robert Smythe, Mr. William Smythe, and Mr. Edward Smythe, who died young: two were knighted by Queen Elizabeth, and two by King James; the eldest was grandfather of the now Lord Strangford; the second had been several times ambassador, and all married into good families, and left great estates to their posterity, which remain to this day. The daughters were Mrs. Fanshawe, your great-grandmother-in-law; the second married Sir John Scott, of Kent; the third married Sir John Davies, of the same county; the fourth married Sir Robert Poynz, of Leicestershire; the fifth married Thomas Butler, of Herald, Esq.; and the sixth married Sir Henry Fanshawe, your grandfather: these all left a numerous posterity but Davies, and this day they are matched into very considerable families. [Footnote: Lady Fanshawe is not quite correct in her account of the Smythe family, and the statements in Peerages are equally erroneous. Thomas Smythe, of Ostenhanger, in Kent, Farmer of the Customs to Philip and Mary, and to Queen Elizabeth, was the second son of John Smythe, Esq., (whose ancestors were seated at Corsham, in Wiltshire, as early as the 15th century,) by Joan, daughter of Robert Brounker, ancestor of the celebrated Viscount Brounker. Customer Smythe died in 1591, and had by Alice, daughter and heiress of Sir Andrew Judde, Lord Mayor of London, and one of the representatives of Archbishop Chicheley, seven sons and six daughters, 1. Andrew, who died young. 2. Sir John, of Ostenhanger, father of Sir Thomas Smythe, K.B., who married Lady Barbara Sydney, daughter of Robert first Earl of Leicester, K.G., was created Viscount Strangford, in Ireland, in 1628, and was the ancestor of Percy Clinton Sydney Smythe, sixth and present Viscount Strangford and first Baron Penshurst, G.C.B. 3. Henry Smythe, of Corsham. 4. Sir Thomas Smythe, of Bidborough, in the county of Kent, ambassador to Russia in 1604, whose male descendants became extinct on the death of Sir Stafford Sydney Smythe, Chief Baron of the Exchequer, in 1778. 5. Sir Richard Smythe, of Leeds Castle, in Kent, whose son, Sir John, dying issueless, in 1632, his sisters became his co-heiresses. 6. Robert Smythe, of Highgate, who left issue. 7. Symon Smythe, killed at the siege of Cadiz in 1597. Of the daughters of Customer Smythe, Mary married Robert Davye, of London, Esq.; Ursula married, first, Simon Harding, of London, Esq., and secondly William Butler, of Bidenham, in Bedfordshire, Esq.; Johanna was the wife of Thomas Fanshawe, of Ware Park, Herts, Esq.; Katherine was first the wife of Sir Rowland Hayward, Lord Mayor of London, and secondly of Sir John Scott, of Scott's Hall, in Kent; Alice married Edward Harris, of Woodham, in Essex, Esq.; and Elizabeth, the sixth and youngest daughter, was the wife of Sir Henry Fanshawe, Remembrancer of the Exchequer, father of Sir Richard Fanshawe, the ambassador. Sir ROBERT Poyntz, of Leicestershire, is a mistake of Lady Fanshawe's for Sir JAMES Poyntz, of North Oxenden, in Essex, who married Mary, the sister and co- heiress of Sir John Smythe, son of Sir Richard, of Bidborough, before mentioned, and GRANDDAUGHTER of the Customer.]

Your great-grandfather had by his second wife, Sir Thomas Fanshawe, Clerk of the Crown, and Surveyor-General of King James; to him he gave his manor of Jenkins, in Essex, valued at near two thousand a year.

His second son by the same wife, William, he procured to be Auditor of the Duchy, whose posterity hath in Essex, at Parslowes, about seven or eight hundred pounds a year. His eldest daughter married Sir Christopher Hatton, heir to the Lord Chancellor Hatton; his second married Sir Benjamin Ayloffe, of Brackstead, in Essex; the third married Mr. Bullock Harding, in Derbyshire; all men of very great estates. As your grandfather inherited Ware Park and his office, the flower of his father's estate, so did he of his wisdom and parts; and both were happy in the favour of the princes of that time, for Queen Elizabeth said that your grandfather was the best officer of accounts she had, and a person of great integrity; and your grandfather was the favourite of Prince Henry, and had the Prince lived to be King, had been Secretary of State, as he would often tell him. Mr. Camden speaks much in praise, as you may see, of Sir Henry Fanshawe's garden of Ware Park, none excelling it in flowers, physic herbs, and fruit, in which things he did greatly delight; also he was a great lover of music, and kept many gentlemen that were perfectly well qualified both in that and the Italian tongue, in which he spent some time. He likewise kept several horses of manege, and rid them himself, which he delighted in, and the Prince would say none did it better; he had great honour and generosity in his nature, and to show you a little part of which I will tell you this of him. He had a horse that the then Earl of Exeter was much pleased with, and Sir Henry esteemed, because he deserved it. My Lord, after some apology, desired Sir Henry to let him have his horse and he would give him what he would; he replied, "My Lord, I have no thoughts of selling him but to serve you; I bought him of such a person, and gave so much for him, and that shall be my price to you as I paid, being sixty pieces"; my Lord Exeter said, "'That's too much, but I will give you, Sir Henry, fifty," to which he made no answer; next day my Lord sent a gentleman with sixty pieces, Sir Henry made answer, "'That was the price he paid and once had offered him, my Lord, at, but not being accepted, his price now was eighty"; at the receiving of this answer my Lord Exeter stormed, and sent his servant back with seventy pieces. Sir Henry said, that "since my Lord would not like him at eighty pieces, he would not sell him under a hundred pieces, and if he returned with less he would not sell him at all"; upon which my Lord Exeter sent one hundred pieces, and had the horse. His retinue was great, and that made him stretch his estate, which was near if not full four thousand pounds a year; yet when he died, he left no debt upon his estate. He departed this life at the age of forty-eight years, and lies buried in the chancel, in a vault with his father in the parish church of Ware; he was as handsome and as fine a gentleman as England then had, a most excellent husband, father, friend, and servant to his Prince. He left in the care of my lady his widow, five sons and five daughters. His eldest son succeeded him in his lands and office, and after the restoration of the King, he was made Lord Viscount of Dromore in Ireland; he did engage his person and estate for the crown, and fought in the battle of Edgehill, and this ruined his estate, and was the cause of his sons selling Ware Park; afterwards he tried, by the King's assistance, to be reimbursed, but could not prevail. He was a very worthy, valiant, honest, good-natured gentleman, charitable, and generous, and had excellent natural parts, yet choleric and rash, which was only incommode to his own family: he was a very pretty man, for he was but low, of a sanguine complexion, much a gentleman in his mien and language; he was sixty-nine years of age when he died, and is buried with his ancestors in Ware Church.

He married first the daughter of Sir Giles Allington, by whom he hath a daughter called Anne, who remains a maid to this day; his second wife was Elizabeth, daughter to Sir William Cockain, Lord Mayor of London. She was a very good wife, but not else qualified extraordinary in any thing. She brought him many children, whereof now remain three sons and five daughters.

Thomas, Lord Viscount Fanshawe, his eldest son, died in May 1674; he was a handsome gentleman, of an excellent understanding, and great honour and honesty. He married the daughter and sole heir of Knitton Ferrers, of Bedford-bury, in the county of Hertford, Esq., by whom he had no child. After his father's death he married the daughter of Sir John Evelyn, widow to Sir John Wrey, of Lincolnshire; by this wife he had several children, of which only two survived him, Thomas, now Lord Viscount Fanshawe, and Katherine. His widow is lately married unto my Lord Castleton, of Senbeck, in Yorkshire. He lies buried with his ancestors in the Parish Church of Ware. Your uncle Henry, that was the second, was killed in fighting gallantly in the Low Countries with the English colours in his hand. He was very handsome and a very brave man, beloved and lamented by all who knew him. The third died a bachelor; I knew him not. The fourth is Sir Simon Fanshawe, a gallant gentleman, but more a libertine than any of his family; he married a very fine and good woman, and of a great estate; she was daughter and coheir to Sir William Walter, and widow to Knitton Ferrers, son to Sir John Ferrers, of Hertfordshire.

Your father, Sir Richard Fanshawe, Knight and Baronet, one of the Masters of the Requests, Secretary of the Latin Tongue, Burgess for the University of Cambridge, and one of his Majesty's most honourable Privy Council of England and Ireland, and his Majesty's Ambassador to Portugal and Spain, was the fifth and youngest son. He married me, the eldest daughter of Sir John Harrison, Knight, of Balls, in the county of Hertford; he was married at thirty-five years of age, and lived with me twenty-three years and twenty-nine days; he lies buried in a new vault I purchased of Humphry, Lord Bishop of London, in St. Mary's Chapel in the Church of Ware, near his ancestors, over which I built him a monument.

My dear husband had six sons and eight daughters, born and christened, and I miscarried of six more, three at several times, and once of three sons when I was about half gone my time. Harrison, my eldest son, and Henry, my second son; Richard, my third;

Henry, my fourth; and Richard, my fifth, are all dead; my second lies buried in the Protestant Church-yard in Paris, by the father of the Earl of Bristol; my eldest daughter Anne lies buried in the Parish Church of Tankersley, in Yorkshire, where she died; Elizabeth lies in the Chapel of the French Hospital at Madrid, where she died of a fever at ten days old; my next daughter of her name lies buried in the Parish of Foot's Cray, in Kent, near Frog-Pool, my brother Warwick's house, where she died; and my daughter Mary lies in my father's vault in Hertford, with my first son Henry; my eldest lies buried in the Parish Church of St. John's College in Oxford, where he was born; my second Henry lies in Bengy Church, in Hertfordshire; and my second Richard in the Esperanza in Lisbon in Portugal, he being born ten weeks before my time when I was in that Court. I praise God I have living yourself and four sisters, Katherine unmarried, Margaret married to Vincent Grantham, Esq., of Goltho, in the county of Lincoln, Anne, and Elizabeth.

Now I have shown you the most part of your family by the male line, except Sir Thomas Fanshawe, of Jenkins, who has but one child, and that a daughter, and two brothers, both unmarried. Their father as well as themselves was a worthy honest gentleman and a great sufferer for the Crown, wholly engaging his estate for the maintenance thereof; and so is my cousin John Fanshawe, of Parslowes, in Essex, who hath but two sons, one unmarried by his first wife, who was the daughter of Sir William Kingsmill; and the other is a child whom he had by his last wife, the daughter of my cousin, Thomas Fanshawe, of Jenkins.

I confess I owe Sir Thomas Fanshawe as good a character as I can express, for he fully deserves it, both for his true honours, and most excellent acquired and natural parts; and that which is of me most esteemed, he was your father's intimate friend as well as near kinsman; and during the time of the war he was very kind to us, by assisting us in our wants, which were as great as his supports; which, though, I thank God, I have fully repaid, yet must ever remain obliged for his kindness and the esteem he hath for us.

He married the daughter and heir of Sir Edward Heath, a pretty lady and a good woman; but I must here with thankfulness acknowledge God's bounty to your family, who hath bestowed most excellent wives on most of them, both in person and fortune; but with respect to the rest, I must give with all reverence justly your grandmother the first and best place, who being left a widow at thirty-nine years of age, handsome, with a full fortune, all her children provided for, kept herself a widow, and out of her jointure and revenue purchased six hundred pounds a year for the younger children of her eldest son; besides, she added five hundred pounds a piece to the portions of her younger children, having nine, whereof but one daughter was married before the death of Sir Henry Fanshawe, and she was the second, her name was Mary, married to William Neuce, Esq., of Hadham, in Hertfordshire; the eldest daughter married Sir Capell Bedells, of Hammerton, in Huntingdonshire; the third never married; the fourth married Sir William Boteler, of Teston, in Kent; the fifth died young. Thus you have been made acquainted with most of your nearest relations by your father, except your cousins german, which are the three sons of your uncle, Lord Fanshawe, and William Neuce, Esq., and his two brothers, and Sir Oliver Boteler, and my Lady Campbell, three maiden sisters of hers, and my Lady Levingthorpe, of Blackware, in Hertfordshire. There was more, but they are dead; and so are the most part of them I have named, but their memories will remain as long as their names, for honest, worthy, virtuous men and women, who served God in their generations in their several capacities, and without vanity none exceeded them in their loyalty, which cost them dear, for there were as many fathers, sons, uncles, nephews, and cousins german, and those that matched to them, engaged and sequestered for the Crown in the time of the late rebellion as their revenue made nearly eighty thousand pounds a year, and this I have often seen a list of and know it to be true.

The use of which to you is, that you should not omit your duty to your king and country, nor be less in your industry to exceed at least, not shame, the excellent memory of your ancestors. They were all eminent officers; and that, I believe, keeping them ever employed, made them so good men. I hope in God the like parallel will be in you, which I heartily and daily pray for.

I was born in St. Olave's, Hart-street, London, in a house that my father took of the Lord Dingwall, father to the now Duchess of Ormond, in the year 1625, on our Lady Day,

25th of March. Mr. Hyde, Lady Alston, and Lady Wolstenholme, were my godfather and godmothers. In that house I lived the winter times till I was fifteen years old and three months, with my ever honoured and most dear mother, who departed this life on the 20th day of July, 1640, and now lies buried in Allhallow's Church, in Hertford. Her funeral cost my father above a thousand pounds; and Dr. Howlsworth preached her funeral sermon, in which, upon his own knowledge, he told before many hundreds of people this accident following: that my mother, being sick to death of a fever three months after I was born, which was the occasion she gave me suck no longer, her friends and servants thought to all outward appearance that she was dead, and so lay almost two days and a night, but Dr. Winston coming to comfort my father, went into my mother's room, and looking earnestly on her face, said "she was so handsome, and now looks so lovely, I cannot think she is dead"; and suddenly took a lancet out of his pocket and with it cut the sole of her foot, which bled. Upon this, he immediately caused her to be laid upon the bed again and to be rubbed, and such means as she came to life, and opening her eyes, saw two of her kinswomen stand by her, my Lady Knollys and my Lady Russell, both with great wide sleeves, as the fashion then was, and said, Did not you promise me fifteen years, and are you come again? which they not understanding, persuaded her to keep her spirits quiet in that great weakness wherein she then was; but some hours after she desired my father and Dr. Howlsworth might be left alone with her, to whom she said, "I will acquaint you, that during the time of my trance I was in great quiet, but in a place I could neither distinguish nor describe; but the sense of leaving my girl, who is dearer to me than all my children, remained a trouble upon my spirits. Suddenly I saw two by me, clothed in long white garments, and methought I fell down with my face in the dust; and they asked why I was troubled in so great happiness. I replied, O let me have the same grant given to Hezekiah, that I may live fifteen years, to see my daughter a woman: to which they answered, It is done; and then, at that instant, I awoke out of my trance;" and Dr. Howlsworth did there affirm, that that day she died made just fifteen years from that time. My dear mother was of excellent beauty and good understanding, a loving wife, and most tender mother; very pious, and charitable to that degree, that she relieved, besides the offals of the table, which she constantly gave to the poor, many with her own hand daily out of her purse, and dressed many wounds of miserable people, when she had health, and when that failed, as it did often, she caused her servants to supply that place.

She left behind her three sons, all much older than myself. The eldest, John, married three wives: by his last, who was the daughter of Mr. Ludlow, a very ancient and noble family, he left two daughters, who are both unmarried. My second brother, William, died at Oxford with a bruise on his side, caused by the fall of his horse, which was shot under him, as he went out with a party of horse against a party of the Earl of Essex, in 1643. He was a very good and gallant young man; and they are the very words the king said of him, when he was told of his death: he was much lamented by all who knew him. The third, Abraham, hath left no issue; I was the fourth, and my sister Margaret, the fifth, who married Sir Edmund Turner, of South Stock, in Lincolnshire, a worthy pious man.

My father, in his old age, married again, the daughter of Mr. Shatbolt, of Hertfordshire, and had by her a son, Richard, and a daughter, Mary. The son married the eldest daughter of the now Lord Grandison, and the daughter married the eldest son of Sir Rowland Lytton, of Knebworth, in Hertfordshire. My father lived to see them both married; and enjoyed a firm health, until above eighty years of age. He was a handsome gentleman of great natural parts, a great accomptant, vast memory, an incomparable penman, of great integrity and service to his prince; had been a member of several Parliaments; a good husband and father, especially to me, who never can sufficiently praise God for him, nor acknowledge his most tender affection and bounty to me and mine; but as in duty bound, I will for ever say, none had ever a kinder and better father than myself. He died on the 28th day of September, 1670; and lies buried by my mother in his own vault in Allhallows Church, in Hertford.

My father was born at Bemond, in Lancashire; the twelfth son of his father, whose mother was the daughter of Mr. Hippom, cousin german to the old Countess of Rivers. I have little knowledge of my father's relations more than the families of Aston, Irland, Sandis,

Bemond, and Curwen, who brought him to London and placed him with my Lord Treasurer Salisbury, then Secretary of State, who sent him into Sir John Wolstenholm's family, and gave him a small place in the Custom- house, to enable him for the employment. He, being of good parts and great capacity, in some time raised himself, by God's help, to get a very great estate, for I have often heard him say that, besides his education, he never had but twenty marks, which his father gave him when he came to London, and that was all he ever had for a portion. He made it appear with great truth that, during the time of the war, he lost by the rebels above one hundred and thirty thousand pounds, and yet he left his son sixteen hundred pounds a year in land, and gave his daughter above twenty thousand pounds.

Now it is necessary to say something of my mother's education of me, which was with all the advantages that time afforded, both for working all sorts of fine works with my needle, and learning French, singing, lute, the virginals and dancing, and notwithstanding I learned as well as most did, yet was I wild to that degree, that the hours of my beloved recreation took up too much of my time, for I loved riding in the first place, running, and all active pastimes; in short, I was that which we graver people call a hoyting girl; but to be just to myself, I never did mischief to myself or people, nor one immodest word or action in my life, though skipping and activity was my delight, but upon my mother's death, I then began to reflect, and, as an offering to her memory, I flung away those childnesses that had formerly possessed me, and, by my father's command, took upon me charge of his house and family, which I so ordered by my excellent mother's example as found acceptance in his sight. I was very well beloved by all our relations and my mother's friends, whom I paid a great respect to, and I ever was ambitious to keep the best company, which I have done, I thank God, all the days of my life. My father and mother were both great lovers and honourers of clergymen, but all of Cambridge, and chiefly Doctor Bamberge, Doctor Howlsworth, Broanbricke, Walley, and Mickelthite, and Sanderson, with many others. We lived in great plenty and hospitality, but no lavishness in the least, nor prodigality, and, I believe, my father never drank six glasses of wine in his life in one day.

About 1641, my brother, William Harrison, was chosen Burgess of ——, and sat in the Commons' House of Parliament, but not long, for when the King set up his standard he went with him to Nottingham; yet he, during his sitting, undertook that my father should lend one hundred and fifty thousand pounds to pay the Scots who had then entered England, and, as it seems, were to be both paid and prayed to go home, but afterwards their plague infected the whole nation, as to all our sorrows we know, and that debt of my father's remained to him until the restoration of the King. In 1642 my father was taken prisoner at his house, called Montague House, in Bishopgate Street, and threatened to be sent on board a ship with many more of his quality, and then they plundered his house, but he getting loose, under pretence to fetch some writings they demanded in his hands concerning the public revenue, he went to Oxford in 1643, and thereupon the Long Parliament, of which he was a member for the town of Lancaster, plundered him out of what remained, and sequestered his whole estate, which continued out of his possession until the happy restoration of the King.

My father commanded my sister and myself to come to him to Oxford where the Court then was, but we, that had till that hour lived in great plenty and great order, found ourselves like fishes out of the water, and the scene was so changed, that we knew not at all how to act any part but obedience, for, from as good a house as any gentleman of England had, we came to a baker's house in an obscure street, and from rooms well furnished, to lie in a very bad bed in a garret, to one dish of meat, and that not the best ordered, no money, for we were as poor as Job, nor clothes more than a man or two brought in their cloak bags: we had the perpetual discourse of losing and gaining towns and men; at the windows the sad spectacle of war, sometimes plague, sometimes sicknesses of other kind, by reason of so many people being packed together, as, I believe, there never was before of that quality; always in want, yet I must needs say that most bore it with a martyr-like cheerfulness. For my own part, I began to think we should all, like Abraham, live in tents all the days of our lives. The King sent my father a warrant for a baronet, but he returned it with thanks, saying he had too much honour of his knighthood which his Majesty had honoured him with some years before, for the fortune he now possessed: but as in a rock the turbulence of the waves disperses the splinters of the rock, so it was my lot, for having buried my dear brother, William Harrison, in Exeter College Chapel, I then married your dear father in 1644 in Wolvercot Church, two miles from Oxford, upon the 18th day of May. None was at our wedding but my dear father, who, at my mother's desire, gave me her wedding-ring, with which I was married, and my sister Margaret, and my brother and sister Boteler, Sir Edward Hyde, afterwards Lord Chancellor, and Sir Geoffry Palmer, the King's Attorney. Before I was married, my husband was sworn Secretary of War to the Prince, now our King, with a promise from Charles I. to be preferred as soon as occasion offered it, but both his fortune and my promised portion, which was made 10,000 pounds, were both at that time in expectation, and we might truly be called merchant adventurers, for the stock we set up our trading with did not amount to twenty pounds betwixt us; but, however, it was to us as a little piece of armour is against a bullet, which if it be right placed, though no bigger than a shilling, serves as well as a whole suit of armour; so our stock bought pen, ink and paper, which was your father's trade, and by it, I assure you, we lived better than those that were born to 2000 pounds a year as long as he had his liberty. Here stay till I have told you your father's life until I married him.

He was but seven years old when his father died, and his mother, my Lady, designed him for the law, having bred him first with that famous schoolmaster Mr. Farnaby, and then under the tuition of Dr. Beale, in Jesus College in Cambridge, from whence, being a most excellent Latinist, he was admitted into the Inner Temple; but it seemed so crabbed a study, and disagreeable to his inclinations, that he rather studied to obey his mother than to make any progress in the law. Upon the death of his mother, whom he dearly loved and honoured, he went into France to Paris, where he had three cousins german, Lord Strangford, Sir John Baker of Kent, and my cousin Thornhill. The whole stock he carried with him was eighty pieces of gold, and French silver to the value of five pounds in his pocket; his gold was quilted in his doublet; he went by post to lodgings in the Fauxbourg St. Germain, with an intent to rest that night, and the next day to find out his kindred; but the devil, that never sleeps, so ordered it, that two friars entered the chamber wherein he was, and welcoming him, being his countrymen, invited him to play, he innocently only intending diversion, till his supper was ready; but that was not their design, for having engaged him, they left him not as long as he was worth a groat, which when they discovered, they gave him five pieces of his money until he could recruit himself by his friends, which he did the next day: and from that time forward never played for a piece. It came to pass, that seven years after, my husband being in Huntingdonshire, at a bowling-green, with Sir Capel Bedells, and many other persons of quality, one in the company was called Captain Taller. My husband, who had a very quick and piercing eye, marked him much, as knowing his face, and found, through his peruke wig, and scarlet cloak and buff suit, that his name was neither Captain nor Taller, but the honest Jesuit called Friar Sherwood, that had cheated him of the greatest part of his money, and after had lent him the five pieces; so your father went to him, and gave him his five pieces, and said, 'Father Sherwood, I know you, and you know this:' at which he was extremely surprised, and begged of your father not to discover him, for his life was in danger. After a year's stay in Paris, he travelled to Madrid in Spain, there to learn that language; at the same time, for that purpose, went the late Earl of Caernarvon, and my Lord of Bedford, and Sir John Berkeley, and several other gentlemen. Afterwards, having spent some years abroad, he returned to London, and gave so good an account of his travels, that he was about the year 1630 made Secretary of the Embassy, when my Lord Aston went Ambassador. During your father's travels, he had spent a considerable part of his stock, which his father and mother left him: in those days, where there were so many younger children, it was inconsiderable, being 50 pounds a year, and 1,500 pounds in money. Upon the return of the ambassador, your father was left resident until Sir Arthur Hopton went Ambassador, and then he came home about the year 1637 or 1638; and I must tell you here of an accident your father had coming out of Spain in this journey post: he going into a bed for some few hours to refresh himself, in a village five leagues from Madrid, he slept so soundly, that notwithstanding the house was on fire, and all the people of the village there, he never waked; but the honesty of the owners was such, that they carried him, and set him asleep upon a piece of timber on the highway; and there he awaked, and found his portmanteau and clothes by him, without the least loss, which is extraordinary, considering the profession of his landlord, who had at that time his house burnt to the ground. After being here a year or two, and no preferment coming, Secretary Windebank calling him Puritan, being his enemy, because himself was a Papist, he was, by his elder brother, put into the place of the King's Remembrancer, absolutely, with this proviso, that he should be accountable for the use of the income; but if in seven years he would pay 8,000 pounds for it to his brother, then it should be his, with the whole revenue of it; but the war breaking out presently after, put an end to this design; for, being the King's sworn servant, he went to the King at Oxford, as well as his fellows, to avoid the fury of this madness of the people, where, having been almost a year, we married, as I said before; and I will continue my discourse where we left.

Now we appear on the stage, to act what part God designed us; and as faith is the evidence of things not seen, so we, upon so righteous a cause, cheerfully resolved to suffer what that would drive us to, which afflictions were neither few nor small, as you will find. This year the Prince had an established Council, which were the Earl of Berkshire, Earl of Bradford, Lord Capel, Lord Colepeper, Lord Hopton, and Sir Edward Hyde, Chancellor of the Exchequer. My husband was then, as I said, newly entered into his office of secretary of the Council of War, and the King would have had him then to have been sworn his Highness's Secretary, but the Queen, who was then no friend to my husband, because he had formerly made Secretary Windebank appear in his colours, who was one of her Majesty's favourites, wholly obstructed that then, and placed with the Prince Sir Robert Long, for whom she had a great kindness; but the consequence will show the man.

The beginning of March 1645, your father went to Bristol with his new master, and this was his first journey: I then lying-in of my first son, Harrison Fanshawe, who was born on the 22nd of February, he left me behind him. As for that, it was the first time we had parted a day since we married; he was extremely afflicted, even to tears, though passion was against his nature; but the sense of leaving me with a dying child, which did die two days after, in a garrison town, extremely weak, and very poor, were such circumstances as he could not bear with, only the argument of necessity; and, for my own part, it cost me so dear, that I was ten weeks before I could go alone; but he, by all opportunities, wrote to me to fortify myself, and to comfort me in the company of my father and sister, who were both with me, and that as soon as the Lords of the Council had their wives come to them I should come to him, and that I should receive the first money he got, and hoped it would be suddenly. By the help of God, with these cordials I recovered my former strength by little and little, nor did I in my distressed condition lack the conversation of many of my relations then in Oxford, and kindnesses of very many of the nobility and gentry, both for goodness sake, and because your father being there in good employment, they found him serviceable to themselves or friends, which friendships none better distinguished between his place and person than your father.

It was in May 1645, the first time I went out of my chamber and to church, where, after service, Sir William Parkhurst, a very honest gentleman, came to me, and said he had a letter for me from your father and fifty pieces of gold, and was coming to bring them to me. I opened first my letter, and read those inexpressible joys that almost overcame me, for he told me I should the Thursday following come to him, and to that purpose he had sent me that money, and would send two of his men with horses, and all accommodation both for myself, my father, and sister, and that Lady Capell and Lady Bradford would meet me on the way; but that gold your father sent me when I was ready to perish, did not so much revive me as his summons. I went immediately to walk, or at least to sit in the air, being very weak, in the garden of St. John's College, and there, with my good father, communicated my joy, who took great pleasure to hear of my husband's good success and likewise of his journey to him. We, all of my household being present, heard drums beat in the highway, under the garden wall. My father asked me if I would go up upon the mount to see the soldiers march, for it was Sir Charles Lee's company of foot, an acquaintance of ours; I said yes, and went up, leaning my back to a tree that grew on the mount. The commander seeing us there, in compliment gave us a volley of shot, and one of their muskets being loaded, shot a brace of bullets not two inches above my head as I leaned to the tree, for which mercy and deliverance I praise God. And next week we were all on our journey for Bristol very merry, and thought that now all things would mend, and the worst of my misfortunes past, but little thought I to leap into the sea that would toss me until it had racked me; but we were to ride all night by agreement, for fear of the enemy surprising us as they passed, they quartering in the way. About nightfall having travelled about twenty miles, we discovered a troop of horse coming towards us, which proved to be Sir Marmaduke Rawdon, a worthy commander and my countryman: he told me, that hearing I was to pass by his garrison, he was come out to conduct me, he hoped as far as was danger, which was about twelve miles: with many thanks we parted, and having refreshed ourselves and horses, we set forth for Bristol, where we arrived on the 20th of May.

My husband had provided very good lodgings for us, and as soon as he could come home from the Council, where he was at my arrival, he with all expressions of joy received me in his arms, and gave me a hundred pieces of gold, saying, "I know thou that keeps my heart so well, will keep my fortune, which from this time I will ever put into thy hands as God shall bless me with increase." And now I thought myself a perfect queen, and my husband so glorious a crown, that I more valued myself to be called by his name than born a princess, for I knew him very wise and very good, and his soul doted on me; upon which confidence I will tell you what happened. My Lady Rivers, a brave woman, and one that had suffered many thousand pounds loss for the King, and whom I had a great reverence for, and she a kindness for me as a kinswoman, in discourse she tacitly commended the knowledge of state affairs, and that some women were very happy in a good understanding thereof, as my Lady Aubigny, Lady Isabel Thynne, and divers others, and yet none was at first more capable than I; that in the night she knew there came a post from Paris from the Queen, and that she would be extremely glad to hear what the Queen commanded the King in order to his affairs; saying, if I would ask my husband privately, he would tell me what he found in the packet, and I might tell her. I that was young and innocent, and to that day had never in my mouth what news, began to think there was more in inquiring into public affairs than I thought of, and that it being a fashionable thing would make me more beloved of my husband, if that had been possible, than I was. When my husband returned home from Council, after welcoming him, as his custom ever was he went with his handful of papers into his study for an hour or more; I followed him; he turned hastily, and said, "What wouldst thou have, my life?" I told him, I had heard the Prince had received a packet from the Queen, and I guessed it was that in his hand, and I desired to know what was in it; he smilingly replied, "My love, I will immediately come to thee, pray thee go, for I am very busy." When he came out of his closet I revived my suit; he kissed me, and talked of other things. At supper I would eat nothing; he as usual sat by me, and drank often to me, which was his custom, and was full of discourse to company that was at table. Going to bed I asked again, and said I could not believe he loved me if he refused to tell me all he knew; but he answered nothing, but stopped my mouth with kisses. So we went to bed, I cried, and he went to sleep. Next morning early, as his custom was, he called to rise, but began to discourse with me first, to which I made no reply; he rose, came on the other side of the bed and kissed me, and drew the curtains softly and went to Court. When he came home to dinner, he presently came to me as was usual, and when I had him by the hand, I said, 'Thou dost not care to see me troubled'; to which he taking me in his arms, answered, 'My dearest soul, nothing upon earth can afflict me like that, and when you asked me of my business, it was wholly out of my power to satisfy thee, for my life and fortune shall be thine, and every thought of my heart in which the trust I am in may not be revealed, but my honour is my own, which I cannot preserve if I communicate the Prince's affairs; and pray thee with this answer rest satisfied.' So great was his reason and goodness, that upon consideration it made my folly appear to me so vile, that from that day until the day of his death I never thought fit to ask him any business but what he communicated freely to me in order to his estate or family. My husband grew much in the Prince's favour; and Mr. Long not being suffered to execute the business of his place, as the Council suspected that he held private intelligence with the Earl of Essex, which when he perceived he went into the enemy's quarters, and so to London, and then into France, full of complaints of the Prince's Council to the Queen-Mother, and when he was gone your father supplied his place.

About July this year, [1645,] the plague increased so fast in Bristol, that the Prince and all his retinue went to Barnstaple, which is one of the finest towns in England; and your father and I went two days after the Prince; for during all the time I was in the Court I never journeyed but either before him, or when he was gone, nor ever saw him but at church, for it was not in those days the fashion for honest women, except they had business, to visit a man's Court. I saw there at Mr. Palmer's, where we lay, who was a merchant, a parrot above a hundred years old. They have, near this town, a fruit called a massard, like a cherry, but different in taste, and makes the best pies with their sort of cream I ever eat. My Lady Capell here left us, and with a pass from the Earl of Essex, went to London with her eldest daughter, now Marquesse of Worcester. Sir Allan Apsley was governor of the town, and we had all sorts of good provision and accommodation; but the Prince's affairs calling him from that place, we went to Launceston, in Cornwall, and thither came very many gentlemen of that county to do their duties to his Highness: they were generally loyal to the crown and hospitable to their neighbours, but they are of a crafty and censorious nature, as most are so far from London. That country hath great plenty, especially of fish and fowl, but nothing near so fat and sweet as within forty miles of London. We were quartered at Truro, twenty miles beyond Launceston, in which place I had like to have been robbed. One night having with me but seven or eight persons, my husband being then at Launceston with his master, somebody had discovered that my husband had a little trunk of the Prince's in keeping, in which were some jewels that tempted them us to assay; but, praised be God, I defended, with the few servants I had, the house so long that help came from the town to my rescue, which was not above a flight shot from the place where I dwelt; and the next day upon my notice my husband sent me a guard by his Highness's command. From thence the Court removed to Pendennis Castle, some time commanded by Sir Nicholas Slanning, who lost his life bravely in the King's service [Footnote: He was killed at the siege of Bristol.], and left an excellent name behind him. In this place came Sir John Granville into his Highness's service, and was made a gentleman of his bedchamber. His father was a very honest gentleman, and lost his life in the King's service; and his uncle, Sir Richard, was a good commander but a little too severe. I was at Penzance with my father, and in the same town was my brother Fanshawe and his lady and children. My father and that family embarked for Morlaix, in Brittanny, with my father's new wife, which he had then married out of that family. My cousin Fanshawe, of Jenkins, and his eldest son, being with them, went also over, but being in a small vessel of that port and surprised with a great storm, they had all like to have been cast away, which forced them to land in a little creek, two leagues from Morlaix, upon the 28th of March, 1646; and five days after the Prince and all his council embarked themselves in a ship called the Phoenix, for the Isles of Scilly. They went from the Land's-end, and so did we; being accompanied with many gentlemen of that country, among whom was Sir Francis Basset, Governor of the Mount, an honest gentleman, and so were all his family; and in particular we received great civility from them. But we left our house and furniture with Captain Bluet, who promised to keep them until such a time as we could dispose of them; but when we sent, he said he had been plundered of them, notwithstanding it was well known he lost nothing of his own. At that time this loss went deep with us, for we lost to the value of 200 pounds and more. But, as the proverb saith, an evil chance seldom comes alone: we having put all our present estate into two trunks, and carried them aboard with us in a ship commanded by Sir Nicholas Crispe, whose skill and honesty the master and seamen had no opinion of, my husband was forced to appease their mutiny which his miscarriage caused; and taking out money to pay the seamen, that night following they broke open one of our trunks, and took out a bag of 60 pounds and a quantity of gold lace, with our best clothes and linen, with all my combs, gloves, and ribbons, which amounted to near 300 pounds more. The next day, after having been pillaged, and extremely sick and big with child, I was set on shore almost dead in the island of Scilly. When we had got to our quarters near the Castle, where the Prince lay, I went immediately to bed, which was so vile, that my footman ever lay in a better, and we had but three in the whole house, which consisted of four rooms, or rather partitions, two low rooms and two little lofts, with a ladder to go up: in one of these they kept dried fish, which was his trade, and in this my husband's two clerks lay, one there was for my sister, and one for myself, and one amongst the rest of the servants. But, when I waked in the morning, I was so cold I knew not what to do, but the daylight discovered that my bed was near swimming with the sea, which the owner told us afterwards it never did so but at spring tide. With this, we were destitute of clothes,—and meat, and fuel, for half the Court to serve them a month was not to be had in the whole island; and truly we begged our daily bread of God, for we thought every meal our last. The Council sent for provisions to France, which served us, but they were bad, and a little of them. Then, after three weeks and odd days, we set sail for the Isle of Jersey, where we safely arrived, praised be God, beyond the belief of all the beholders from that island; for the pilot not knowing the way into the harbour, sailed over the rocks, but being spring tide, and by chance high water, God be praised, his Highness and all of us came safe ashore through so great a danger. Sir George Carteret was Lieutenant-Governor of the island, under my Lord St. Albans: a man formerly bred a sea-boy, and born in that island, the brother's son of Sir Philip Carteret, whose younger daughter he afterwards married. He endeavoured, with all his power, to entertain his Highness and Court with all plenty and kindness possible, both which the island afforded, and what was wanting, he sent for out of France.

There are in this island two castles, both good, but St. Mary's is best, and hath the largest reception. There are many gentlemen's houses, at which we were entertained. They have fine walks along to their doors, double elms or oaks, which is extremely pleasant, and their ordinary highways are good walks, by reason of the shadow. The whole place is grass, except some small parcels where corn is grown. The chiefest employment is knitting; they neither speak English nor good French; they are a cheerful, good-natured people, and truly subject to the present government. We quartered at a widow's house in the market-place, Madame De Pommes, a stocking merchant: here I was upon the 7th of March, [Footnote: Query, May or June. She did not arrive in Jersey until April.] 1646, delivered of my second child, a daughter, christened Anne. And now there began great disputes about the Prince, for the Queen would have him to Paris, to which end she sent many letters and messengers to his Highness and Council, who were for the most part against his going, both to the Queen his mother, and his going to France, for reasons of state, but the Queen having an excellent solicitor in the Lord Colepeper, it was resolved by his Highness to go: upon which Lord Capell, Lord Hopton, and the Chancellor staid at Jersey, and with them my husband, whose employment ceased when his master went out of his father's kingdom;—not that your father sided with either party of the Council, but having no inclination at that time to go to the Court, and because his brother, Lord Fanshawe, was desperately sick at Caen, he intended to stay some time with him. About the beginning of July, the Prince, accompanied with the Earl of Bradford, a soldier of fortune, and Lord Colepeper, and the Earl of Berkshire, and most of his servants, went to Cotanville, and from thence to Paris, where he remained some little time by his mother the Queen's council, and afterwards went into Holland. Your father and I remained fifteen days in Jersey, and resolved that he would remain with his brother in Caen, whilst he sent me into England, whither my father was gone a month before, to see if I could procure a sum of money. The beginning of August we took our leave of the governor's family, and left our child with a nurse under the care of the Lady Carteret; [Footnote: It was apparently this Lady, of whom Pepys observes, 30th June, 1662. "Told my Lady Carteret, how my Lady Fanshawe is fallen out with her only for speaking in behalf of the French: which my Lady wonders at, they having been formerly like sisters."—Diary, vol. i. p. 284.] and in four days we came to Caen, and myself, sister, and maid went from Mr. Fanborne's house, where my brother and all his family lodged, aboard a small merchantman that lay in the river; and upon the 30th of August, I arrived in the Cowes, near Southampton, to which place I went that night, and came to London two days after. This was the first time I had taken a journey without your father, and the first manage of business he ever put into my hands, in which I thank God I had good success; for, lodging in Fleet Street, at Mr. Eates, the Watchmaker, with my sister Boteler, I procured by the means of Colonel Copley, a great Parliament-man, whose wife had formerly been obliged to our family, a pass for your father to come and compound for 300 pounds which was a part of my fortune, but it was only a pretence, for your grandfather was obliged to compound for it, and deliver it us free. And when your father was come, he was very private in London; for he was in daily fears to be imprisoned before he could raise money to go back again to his master, who was not then in a condition to maintain him. Thus upon thorns he stayed the October 1647. In the October before, 1646, my brother Richard Harrison was born; and this year my sister Boteler married Sir Philip Warwick, her second husband; for her first, Sir William Boteler, was killed at Cropley-bridge, commanding a part of the King's army: he was a most gallant, worthy, honest gentleman.

The 30th of July I was delivered of a son, called Henry, in lodgings in Portugal-row, Lincoln's-inn-fields. This was a very sad time for us all of the King's party, for by the folly, to give it no worse name, of Sir John Berkeley, since Lord Berkeley, and Mr. John Ashburnham, of the King's bedchamber, who were drawn in by the cursed crew of the then standing army for the Parliament to persuade the King to leave Hampton Court, to which they had then carried him, and to make his escape, which design failing, as the plot was laid, he was tormented and afterwards barbarously and shamefully murdered, as all the world knows.

During his stay at Hampton Court, my husband was with him, to whom he was pleased to talk much of his concerns, and give him there credentials for Spain, with private instructions, and letters for his service; but God for our sins disposed his Majesty's affairs otherwise. I went three times to pay my duty to him, both as I was the daughter of his servant, and wife of his servant. The last time I ever saw him, when I took my leave, I could not refrain weeping: when he had saluted me, I prayed to God to preserve his Majesty with long life and happy years; he stroked me on the cheek, and said, 'Child, if God pleaseth, it shall be so, but both you and I must submit to God's will, and you know in what hands I am'; then turning to your father, he said, 'Be sure, Dick, to tell my son all that I have said, and deliver those letters to my wife; pray God bless her! I hope I shall do well'; and taking him in his arms, said, 'Thou hast ever been an honest man, and I hope God will bless thee, and make thee a happy servant to my son, whom I have charged in my letter to continue his love, and trust to you'; adding, 'I do promise you that if ever I am restored to my dignity I will bountifully reward you both for your service and sufferings.' Thus did we part from that glorious sun, that within a few months after was murdered, to the grief of all Christians that were not forsaken by God.

The October, as I told you, my husband and I went into France, by the way of Portsmouth, where, walking by the sea side about a mile from our lodgings, two ships of the Dutch, then in war with England, shot bullets at us so near that we heard them whiz by us; at which I called to my husband to make haste back, and began to run, but he altered not his pace, saying, 'If we must be killed, it were as good to be killed walking as running.' But, escaping, we embarked the next day; and that journey fetched home our girl we had left in Jersey; and my husband was forced to come out of France to Hamerton, in Huntingdonshire, to my sister Bedell's, to the wedding of his nephew, the last Lord Thomas Fanshawe, who then married the daughter of Ferrers: as I have said before, she was a very great fortune, and a most excellent woman, and brought up some time after her mother's death with my sister Bedell.

About two months after this, in June, I was delivered of a son on the 8th day, 1648. The latter end of July I went to London, leaving my little boy Richard at nurse with his brother at Hartingfordbury. It happened to be the very day after that the Lord Holland was taken prisoner at St. Neot, and Lord Francis Villiers was killed; and as we passed through the town, we saw Colonel Montague, afterwards Earl of Sandwich, spoiling the town for the Parliament and himself. Coming to London, I went to welcome the Marchioness of Ormond to town, that then was come out of France, who received me with great kindness, as she ever had done before, and told me she must love me for many reasons, and one was, that we were both born in one chamber: when I left her, she presented me with a ruby ring set with two diamonds, which she prayed me to wear for her sake, and I have it to this day.

In the month of September my husband was commanded by the Prince to wait on him in the Downs, where he was with a very considerable fleet; but the fleet was divided, part being for the King, and part for the Parliament. They were resolved to fight that day, which if they had, would have been the most cruel fight that ever England knew; but God by his will parted them by a storm, and afterwards it was said, Lord Colepeper, and one Low, a surgeon, that was a reputed knave, so ordered the business, that for money the fleet was

27

betrayed to the enemy. During this time my husband wrote me a letter, from on board the Prince's ship, full of concern for me, believing they should engage on great odds; but, if he should lose his life, advised me to patience, and this with so much love and reason, that my heart melts to this day when I think of it; but, God be praised, he was reserved for better things.

In December [Footnote: This must be a mistake for NOVEMBER; for in September he was on board the fleet in the Downs, and after passing SIX WEEKS IN PARIS, he went to Calais with Lady Fanshawe on the 25th of DECEMBER, 1649. The date of the year is also erroneous, as it is evident from the context that it was 1648.] my husband went to Paris on his master's business, and sent for me from London: I carried him 300 pounds of his money. During our stay at Paris, I was highly obliged to the Queen-Mother of England. We passed away six weeks with great delight in good company; my Lady Norton, that was governess to the Lady Henrietta, Charles the First's youngest daughter, was very kind. I had the honour of her company, both in my own lodging and in the Palace Royal, where she attended her charge; likewise my Lady Danby, and her daughter, my Lady Guilford, with many others of our nation, both in the Court and out of it; amongst whom was Mr. Waller, the poet, and his wife: they went with us to Calais, upon the 25th of December, 1649. I, with my husband, kissed the Queen-Mother's hand, who promised her favour, with much grace, to us both, and sent letters to the King, then in Holland, by my husband. From her Majesty we waited on the Princes, and afterwards took our leave of all that Court.

When we came to Calais, we met the Earl of Strafford and Sir Kenelm Digby, with some others of our countrymen. We were all feasted at the Governor's of the castle, and much excellent discourse passed; but, as was reason, most share was Sir Kenelm Digby's, who had enlarged somewhat more in extraordinary stories than might be averred, and all of them passed with great applause and wonder of the French then at table; but the concluding one was, that barnacles, a bird in Jersey, was first a shell-fish in appearance, and from that, sticking upon old wood, became in time a bird. After some consideration, they unanimously burst out into laughter, believing it altogether false; and, to say the truth, it was the only thing true he had discoursed with them: that was his infirmity, though otherwise a person of most excellent parts, and a very fine-bred gentleman.

My husband thought it convenient to send me into England again, there to try what sums I could raise, both for his subsistence abroad and mine at home; and though nothing was so grievous to us both as parting, yet the necessity both of the public and your father's private affairs, obliged us often to yield to the trouble of absence, as at this time. I took my leave with sad heart, and embarked myself in a hoy for Dover, with Mrs. Waller and my sister Margaret Harrison, and my little girl Nan; but a great storm arising, we had like to be cast away, the vessel being half full of water, and we forced to land at Deal, every one carried upon men's backs, and we up to the middle in water, and very glad to escape so. About this time the Prince of Orange was born. [Footnote: This is an error, as he was born on the 4th of November, 1650.]

My husband went from thence by Flanders into Holland to his master; and, in February following, your father was sent into Ireland by the King, there to receive such monies as Prince Rupert could raise by the fleet he commanded of the King's; but a few months put an end to that design, though it had a very good aspect in the beginning, which made my husband send for me and the little family I had thither. We went by Bristol very cheerfully towards my north star, that only had the power to fix me; and because I had had the good fortune, as I then thought it, to sell 300 pounds a year to him that is now Judge Archer, in Essex, for which he gave me 4000 pounds, which at that time I thought a vast sum; but be it more or less, I am sure it was spent in seven years' time in the King's service, and to this hour I repent it not, I thank God. Five hundred pounds I carried to my husband, the rest I left in my father's agent's hands to be returned as we needed it.

I landed at Youghall, in Munster, as my husband directed me, in hopes to meet me there; but I had the discomfort of a very hazardous voyage, and the absence of your father, he then being upon business at Cork. So soon as he heard I was landed, he came to me, and with mutual joy we discoursed those things that were proper to entertain us both; and thus, for six months, we lived so much to our satisfaction, that we began to think of making our abode there during the war, for the country was fertile, and all provisions cheap, and the houses good, and we were placed in Red Abbey, a house of Dean Boyle's in Cork, and my Lord of Ormond had a very good army, and the country seemingly quiet; and, to complete our content, all persons were very civil to us, especially Dean Boyle, Lord Chancellor of Ireland, and Archbishop of Dublin and his family, and the Lord Inchiquin, whose daughter Elkenna I christened in 1650.

But what earthly comfort is exempt from change? for here I heard of the death of my second son, Henry, and, within a few weeks, of the landing of Cromwell, who so hotly marched over Ireland, that the fleet with Prince Rupert was forced to set sail, and within a small time after he lost all his riches, which was thought to be worth hundreds of thousands of pounds, in one of his best ships, commanded by his brother Maurice, who with many a brave man sunk and were all lost in a storm at sea.

We remained some time behind in Ireland, until my husband could receive his Majesty's commands how to dispose of himself. During this time I had, by the fall of a stumbling horse, being with child, broke my left wrist, which, because it was ill-set, put me to great and long pain, and I was in my bed when Cork revolted. By chance that day my husband was gone on business to Kinsale: it was in the beginning of November 1650. [Footnote: These events happened in November 1649.] At midnight I heard the great guns go off, and thereupon I called up my family to rise, which I did as well as I could in that condition. Hearing lamentable shrieks of men, women, and children, I asked at a window the cause; they told me they were all Irish, stripped and wounded, and turned out of the town, and that Colonel Jeffries, with some others, had possessed themselves of the town for Cromwell, Upon this, I immediately wrote a letter to my husband, blessing God's providence that he was not there with me, persuading him to patience and hope that I should get safely out of the town, by God's assistance, and desired him to shift for himself, for fear of a surprise, with promise that I would secure his papers.

So soon as I had finished my letter, I sent it by a faithful servant, who was let down the garden-wall of Red Abbey, and, sheltered by the darkness of the might, he made his escape. I immediately packed up my husband's cabinet, with all his writings, and near 1000 pounds in gold and silver, and all other things both of clothes, linen, and household stuff that were portable, of value; and then, about three o'clock in the morning, by the light of a taper, and in that pain I was in, I went into the market-place, with only a man and maid, and passing through an unruly tumult with their swords in their hands, searched for their chief commander Jeffries, who, whilst he was loyal, had received many civilities from your father. I told him it was necessary that upon that change I should remove, and I desired his pass that would be obeyed, or else I must remain there: I hoped he would not deny me that kindness. He instantly wrote me a pass, both for myself, family, and goods, and said he would never forget the respect he owed your father. With this I came through thousands of naked swords to Red Abbey, and hired the next neighbour's cart, which carried all that I could remove; and myself, sister, and little girl Nan, with three maids and two men, set forth at five o'clock in November, having but two horses amongst us all, which we rid on by turns. In this sad condition I left Red Abbey, with as many goods as were worth 100 pounds which could not be removed, and so were plundered. We went ten miles to Kinsale, in perpetual fear of being fetched back again; but, by little and little, I thank God, we got safe to the garrison, where I found your father the most disconsolate man in the world, for fear of his family, which he had no possibility to assist; but his joys exceeded to see me and his darling daughter, and to hear the wonderful escape we, through the assistance of God, had made.

But when the rebels went to give an account to Cromwell of their meritorious act, he immediately asked them where Mr. Fanshawe was? They replied, he was that day gone to Kinsale. Then he demanded where his papers and his family were? At which they all stared at one another, but made no reply. Their General said, 'It was as much worth to have seized his papers as the town; for I did make account to have known by them what these parts of the country are worth.'

But within a few days we received the King's order, which was, that my husband should, upon sight thereof, go into Spain to Philip IV. and deliver him his Majesty's letters; and by my husband also his Majesty sent letters to my Lord Cottington and Sir Edward

Hyde, his Ambassadors Extraordinary in that Court. Upon this order we went to Macrome to the Lord Clancarty, who married a sister of the Lord Ormond; we stayed there two nights, and at my coming away, after a very noble entertainment, my Lady gave me a great Irish greyhound, and I presented her with a fine besel-stone.

From thence we went to Limerick, where we were entertained by the Mayor and Aldermen very nobly; and the Recorder of the Town was very kind, and in respect they made my husband a freeman of Limerick. There we met the Bishop of Londonderry and the Earl of Roscommon, who was Lord Chancellor of that Kingdom at that time. These two persons with my husband being together writing letters to the King, to give an account of the kingdom, when they were going down stairs from my Lord Roscommon's chamber, striving to hold the candle at the stairs' head, because the privacy of their despatch admitted not a servant to be near, my Lord Roscommon fell down the stairs, and his head fell upon the corner of a stone and broke his skull in three pieces, of which he died five days after, leaving the broad seal of Ireland in your father's hands, until such time as he could acquaint his Majesty with this sad account, and receive orders how to dispose of the seals. This caused our longer stay, but your father and I being invited to my Lord Inchiquin's, there to stay till we heard out of Holland from the King, which was a month before the messenger returned, we had very kind entertainment, and vast plenty of fish and fowl. By this time my Lord Lieutenant the now Duke of Ormond's army was quite dispersed, and himself gone for Holland, and every person concerned in that interest shifting for their lives; and Cromwell went through as bloodily as victoriously, many worthy persons being murdered in cold blood, and their families quite ruined.

From hence we went to the Lady Honor O'Brien's, a lady that went for a maid, but few believed it: she was the youngest daughter of the Earl of Thomond. There we stayed three nights. The first of which I was surprised by being laid in a chamber, when, about one o'clock I heard a voice that wakened me. I drew the curtain, and in the casement of the window, I saw, by the light of the moon, a woman leaning into the window, through the casement, in white, with red hair and pale and ghastly complexion: she spoke loud, and in a tone I had never heard, thrice, 'A horse'; and then, with a sigh more like the wind than breath she vanished, and to me her body looked more like a thick cloud than substance. I was so much frightened, that my hair stood on end, and my night clothes fell off. I pulled and pinched your father, who never woke during the disorder I was in; but at last was much surprised to see me in this fright, and more so when I related the story and showed him the window opened. Neither of us slept any more that night, but he entertained me with telling me how much more these apparitions were usual in this country than in England; and we concluded the cause to be the great superstition of the Irish, and the want of that knowing faith, which should defend them from the power of the Devil, which he exercises among them very much. About five o'clock the lady of the house came to see us, saying she had not been in bed all night, because a cousin O'Brien of her's, whose ancestors had owned that house, had desired her to stay with him in his chamber, and that he died at two o'clock, and she said, 'I wish you to have had no disturbance, for 'tis the custom of the place, that, when any of the family are dying, the shape of a woman appears in the window every night till they be dead. This woman was many ages ago got with child by the owner of this place, who murdered her in his garden and flung her into the river under the window, but truly I thought not of it when I lodged you here, it being the best room in the house.' We made little reply to her speech, but disposed ourselves to be gone suddenly.

By this time my husband had received orders from the King to give the Lord Inchiquin the seals to keep until farther orders from his Majesty. When that business was settled, we went, accompanied by my Lord Inchiquin and his family, four or five miles towards Galway, which he did not by choice, but the plague had been so hot in that city the summer before, that it was almost depopulated, and the haven as much as the town. But your father hearing that, by accident, there was a great ship of Amsterdam bound for Malaga, in Spain, and Cromwell pursuing his conquests at our backs, resolved to fall into the hands of God rather than into the hands of men; and with his family of about ten persons came to the town at the latter end of February, [Footnote: Probably January, as in a subsequent page Lady Fanshawe says, she embarked for Galway in the beginning of

February,] where we found guards placed that none should enter without certificates from whence they came; but understanding that your father came to embark himself for Spain, and that there was a merchant's house taken for us, that was near the sea-side, and one of their best, they told us, if we pleased to alight, they would wait on us to the place; but it was long from thence, and no horses were admitted into the town.

An Irish footman that served us, said, 'I lived here some years and know every street, and likewise know a much nearer way than these men can show you, Sir; therefore come with me, if you please.' We resolved to follow him, and sent our horses to stables in the suburbs: he led us all on the back side of the town, under the walls, over which the people during the plague, which was not yet quite stopped, flung out all their dung, dirt, and rags, and we walked up to the middle of our legs in them, for, being engaged, we could not get back. At last we found the house, by the master standing at the door expecting us, who said, 'You are welcome to this disconsolate city, where you now see the streets grown over with grass, once the finest little city in the world.' And indeed it is easy to think so, the buildings being uniformly built, and a very fine marketplace, and walks arched and paved by the sea-side for their merchants to walk on, and a most noble harbour.

Our house was very clean, only one maid in it besides the master; we had a very good supper provided, and being very weary went early to bed. The owner of this house entertained us with the story of the late Marquis of Worcester, who had been there some time the year before: he had of his own and other friends' jewels to the value of 8000 pounds, which some merchants had lent upon them. My Lord appointed a day for receiving the money upon them and delivering the jewels; being met, he shows them to all these persons, then seals them up in a box, and delivered them to one of these merchants, by consent of the rest, to be kept for one year, and upon the payment of the 8000 pounds by my Lord Marquis to be delivered him.

After my Lord had received the money, he was entertained at all these persons' houses, and nobly feasted with them near a month: he went from thence into France. When the year was expired, they, by letters into France, pressed the payment of this borrowed money several times, alleging they had great necessity of their money to drive their trade with; to which my Lord Marquis made no answer; which did at last so exasperate these men, that they broke open the seals, and opening the box found nothing but rags and stones for their 8000 pounds at which they were highly enraged, and in this case I left them.

At the beginning of February we took ship, and our kind host, with much satisfaction in our company, prayed God to bless us and give us a good voyage, for, said he, 'I thank God you are all gone safe aboard from my house, notwithstanding I have buried nine persons out of my house within these six months'; which saying much startled us, but, God's name be praised, we were all well, and so continued.

Here now our scene was shifted from land to sea, and we left that brave kingdom, fallen, in six or eight months, into a most miserable sad condition, as it hath been many times in most kings' reigns, God knows why! for I presume not to say; but the natives seem to me a very loving people to each other, and constantly false to all strangers, the Spaniards only excepted. The country exceeds in timber and sea-ports, and great plenty of fish, fowl, flesh, and, by shipping, wants no foreign commodities. We pursued our voyage with prosperous winds, but with a most tempestuous master, a Dutchman, which is enough to say, but truly, I think, the greatest beast I ever saw of his kind.

When we had just passed the Straits, we saw coming towards us, with full sails, a Turkish galley well manned, and we believed we should be all carried away slaves, for this man had so laden his ship with goods for Spain, that his guns were useless, though the ship carried sixty guns. He called for brandy; and after he had well drunken, and all his men, which were near two hundred, he called for arms and cleared the deck as well as he could, resolving to fight rather than lose his ship, which was worth thirty thousand pounds. This was sad for us passengers; but my husband bade us be sure to keep in the cabin, and the women not to appear, which would make the Turks think that we were a man-of-war, but if they saw women they would take us for merchants and board us. He went upon the deck, and took a gun and bandoliers, and sword, and, with the rest of the ship's company, stood upon deck expecting the arrival of the Turkish man-of-war. This beast, the Captain, had locked me up in the cabin; I knocked and called long to no purpose, until, at length, the cabin-boy came and opened the door; I, all in tears, desired him to be so good as to give me his blue thrum cap he wore, and his tarred coat, which he did, and I gave him half a crown, and putting them on and flinging away my night clothes, I crept up softly and stood upon the deck by my husband's side, as free from sickness and fear as, I confess, from discretion; but it was the effect of that passion, which I could never master.

By this time the two vessels were engaged in parley, and so well satisfied with speech and sight of each other's forces, that the Turks' man-of-war tacked about, and we continued our course. But when your father saw it convenient to retreat, looking upon me, he blessed himself, and snatched me up in his arms, saying, 'Good God, that love can make this change!' and though he seemingly chid me, he would laugh at it as often as he remembered that voyage. And in the beginning of March we all landed, praised be God, in Malaga, very well, and full of content to see ourselves delivered from the sword and plague, and living in hope that we should one day return happily to our native country; notwithstanding, we thought it great odds, considering how the affairs of the King's three kingdoms stood; but we trusted in the providence of Almighty God, and proceeded.

We were very kindly entertained by the merchants, and by them lodged in a merchant's house, where we had not been with our goods three days, when the vessel that brought us thither, by the negligence of a cabin-boy, was blown up in the harbour, with the loss of above a hundred men and all our lading.

After we had refreshed ourselves some days, we went on our journey towards Madrid, and lodged the first night at Velez Malaga, to which we were accompanied by most of the merchants. The next day we went to Grenada, having passed the highest mountains I ever saw in my life, but under this lieth the finest valley that can be possibly described, adorned with high trees and rich grass, and beautified with a large deep clear river. Over the town and this standeth the goodly vast palace of the King's, called the Alhambra, whose buildings are, after the fashion of the Moors, adorned with vast quantities of jasper-stone; many courts, many fountains, and by reason it is situated on the side of a hill, and not built uniform, many gardens with ponds in them, and many baths made of jasper, and many principal rooms roofed with the mosaic work, which exceeds the finest enamel I ever saw. Here I was showed in the midst of a very large piece of rich embroidery made by the Moors of Grenada, in the middle as long as half a yard of the true Tyrian dye, which is so glorious a colour that it cannot be expressed: it hath the glory of scarlet, the beauty of purple, and is so bright, that when the eye is removed upon any other object it seems as white as snow.

The entry into this great Palace is of stone, for a Porter's-lodge, but very magnificent, through the gate below, which is adorned with figures of forestwork, in which the Moors did transcend. High above this gate was a bunch of keys cut in stone likewise, with this motto: 'Until that hand holds those keys, the Christians shall never possess this Alhambra.' This was a prophecy they had, in which they animated themselves, by reason of the impossibility that ever they should meet. But see, how true there is a time for all things! It happened that when the Moors were besieged in that place by Don Fernando and his Queen Isabella, the King with an arrow out of a bow, which they then used in war, shooting the first arrow as their custom is, cut that part of the stone that holds the keys, which was in fashion of a chain, and the keys falling, remained in the hand underneath. This strange accident preceded but a few days the conquest of the town of Grenada and kingdom.

They have in this place an iron grate, fixed into the side of the hill, that is a rock: I laid my head to the key-hole and heard a noise like the clashing of arms, but could not distinguish other shrill noises I heard with that, but tradition says it could never be opened since the Moors left it, notwithstanding several persons had endeavoured to wrench it open, but that they perished in the attempt. The truth of this I can say no more to; but that there is such a gate, and I have seen it.

After two days we went on our journey; and on the 13th of April 1650, we came to the Court of Madrid, where we were the next day visited by the two English ambassadors, and afterwards by all the English merchants.

Here I was delivered of my first daughter, that was called Elizabeth, upon the 13th of July. She lived but fifteen days, and lies buried in the Chapel of the French Hospital. Your father had great difficulty to carry on his business, without encroaching upon the Extraordinary Ambassador's negotiation, and the performance of his Majesty's commands to show his present necessities, which he was sent to Philip IV. for, in hopes of a present supply of money, which our King then lacked; but finding no good to be done on that errand, he and I, accompanied by Dr. Bell, of Jesus College in Cambridge, who had been his tutor, went a day's journey together towards St. Sebastian, there to embark for France.

While we stayed in this Court we were kindly treated by all the English; and it was no small trouble to your father's tutor to quit his company, but, having undertaken the charge of that family of the ambassador's as their chaplain, he said, he held himself obliged in conscience to stay, and so he did. In a few months after he died there, and lies buried in the garden-house, where they then lived.

Whilst we were in Madrid, there was sent one Askew, as resident from the then Governor of England; he lay in a common eating-house where some travellers used to lie, and being one day at dinner, some young men meeting in the street with Mr. Prodgers, a gentleman belonging to the Lord Ambassador Cottington, and Mr. Sparks, an English merchant, discoursing of news, began to speak of the impudence of that Askew, to come a public minister from rebels to a Court where there were two Ambassadors from his King. This subject being handled with heat, they all resolved to go without more consideration into his lodgings immediately and kill him: they came up to his chamber door, and finding it open, and he sat at dinner, seized him, and so killed him, and went their several ways. Afterwards they found Mr. Sparks in a church for rescue, notwithstanding it was contrary to their religion and laws, and they forced him out from thence, and executed him publicly, their fears of the English power were then so great.

There was at that time the Lord Goring, son to the Earl of Norwich: he had a command under Philip the Fourth of Spain, against the Portuguese: he was generally esteemed a good and great commander, and had been brought up in Holland in his youth, of vast natural parts; for I have heard your father say, he hath dictated to several persons at once that were upon despatches, and all so admirably well, that none of them could be mended. He was exceeding facetious and pleasant company, and in conversation, where good manners were due, the civilest person imaginable, so that he would blush like a girl. He was very tall, and very handsome: he had been married to a daughter of the Earl of Cork, but never had a child by her. His expenses were what he could get, and his debauchery beyond all precedents, which at last lost him that love the Spaniards had for him; and that country not admitting his constant drinking, he fell sick of a hectic fever, in which he turned his religion, and with that artifice could scarce get to keep him whilst he lived in that sickness, or to bury him when he was dead.

We came to St. Sebastian's about the beginning of September, and there hired a small French vessel to carry us to Nantz: we embarked within two days after our coming to this town. I never saw so wild a place, nor were the inhabitants unsuitable, but like to like, which made us hasten away, and I am sure to our cost we found the proverb true, for our haste brought us woe. We had not been a day at sea before we had a storm begun, that continued two days and two nights in a most violent manner; and being in the Bay of Biscay, we had a hurricane that drew the vessel up from the water, which had neither sail nor mast left, and but six men and a boy. Whilst they had hopes of life they ran swearing about like devils, but when that failed them, they ran into holes, and let the ship drive as it would. In this great hazard of our lives we were the beginning of the third night, when God in mercy ceased the storm of a sudden, and there was a great calm, which made us exceeding joyful; but when those beasts, for they were scarce men, that manned the vessel, began to rummage the bark, they could not find their compass anywhere, for the loss of which they began again such horrible lamentations as were as dismal to us as the storm past.

Thus between hope and fear we passed the night, they protesting to us they knew not where they were, and truly we believed them; for with fear and drink I think they were bereaved of their senses. So soon as it was day, about six o'clock, the master cried out, 'The land! the land!' but we did not receive the news with the joy belonging to it, but sighing said, God's will be done! Thus the tide drove us until about five o'clock in the afternoon, and drawing near the side of a small rock that had a creek by it, we ran aground, but the sea was so calm that we all got out without the loss of any man or goods, but the vessel was so shattered that it was not afterwards serviceable: thus, God be praised! we escaped this great danger, and found ourselves near a little village about two leagues from Nantz. We hired there six asses, upon which we rode as many as could by turns, and the rest carried our goods. This journey took us up all the next day, for I should have told you that we stirred not that night, because we sat up and made good cheer; for beds they had none, and we were so transported that we thought we had no need of any, but we had very good fires, and Nantz white wine, and butter, and milk, and walnuts and eggs, and some very bad cheese; and was not this enough, with the escape of shipwreck, to be thought better than a feast? I am sure until that hour I never knew such pleasure in eating, between which we a thousand times repeated what we had spoken when every word seemed to be our last.

As soon as it was day, we began our journey towards Nantz, and by the way we passed by a little poor chapel, at the door of which a friar begged an alms, saying, that he would show us there the greatest wonder in the world. We resolved to go with him. He went before us to the altar, and out of a cupboard, with great devotion, he took a box, and crossing himself he opened it, in that was another of crystal that contained a little silver box; he lifting this crystal box up, cried, 'Behold in this the hem [Footnote: Thus in the MS.; but query if a mistake of the transcriber.] of St. Joseph, which was taken as he hewed his timber!' To which my husband replied, 'Indeed, Father, it is the lightest, considering the greatness, that I ever handled in my life.' The ridiculousness of this, with the simplicity of the man, entertained us till we came to Nantz. We met by the way good grapes and walnuts growing, of which we culled out the best.

Nantz is a passable good town, but decayed: some monasteries in it, but none good nor rich. There was in a nunnery, when I was there, a daughter of Secretary Windebank. There is English provisions, and of all sorts, cheap and good. We hired a boat to carry us up to Orleans, and we were towed up all the river of Loire so far. Every night we went on shore to bed, and every morning carried into the boat wine and fruit, and bread, with some flesh, which we dressed in the boat, for it had a hearth, on which we burnt charcoal: we likewise caught carps, which were the fattest and the best I ever eat in my life. And of all my travels none were, for travel sake as I may call it, so pleasant as this; for we saw the finest cities, seats, woods, meadows, pastures, and champain that I ever saw in my life, adorned with the most pleasant river of Loire; of which, at Orleans, we took our leaves. Arriving, about the middle of November 1650, at Paris, we went, so soon as we could get clothes, to wait on the Queen-Mother and the Princess Henrietta. The Queen entertained us very respectfully, and after many favours done us, and discoursing in private with your father about affairs of state, he received her Majesty's letters to send to the King, who was then on his way to Scotland. We kissed her hand and went to Calais, with resolution that I should go to England, to send my husband more money, for this long journey cost us all we could procure: yet this I will tell you, praised be God for his peculiar grace herein, that your father nor I ever borrowed money nor owed for clothes, nor diet, nor lodging beyond sea in our lives, which was very much, considering the straits we were in many times, and the bad custom our countrymen had that way, which did redound much to the King's dishonour and their own discredit.

When we came to Calais, my husband sent me to England, and staying himself there, intending, as soon as he had received money, to go and live in Holland until such time as it should please Almighty God to enable him again to wait on his Majesty, now in Scotland, both to give him an account of his journey into Spain, as of the rest of his employments since he kissed his hand. But God ordered it otherwise; for the case being that the two parties in Scotland being both unsatisfied with each other's ministers, and Sir E. Hyde and Secretary Nicholas being excepted against, and left in Holland, it was proposed, the state wanting a Secretary for the King, that your father should be immediately sent for, which was done accordingly, and he went with letters and presents from the Princess of Orange, and the Princess Royal.

Here I will show you something of Sir Edward Hyde's nature: he being surprised with this news, and suspecting that my husband might come to a greater power than himself, both because of his parts and integrity, and because himself had been sometimes absent in the Spanish Embassy, he with all the humility possible, and earnest passion, begged my husband to remember the King often of him to his advantage as occasion should serve, and to procure leave that he might wait on the King, promising, with all the oaths that he could express to cause belief, that he would make it his business all the days of his life to serve your father's interest in what condition soever he should be in: thus they parted, with your father's promise to serve him in what he was capable of, upon which account many letters passed between them.

When your father arrived in Scotland, he was received by the King with great expressions of great content; and after he had given an account of his past employment, he was by the King recommended to the York party, who received him very kindly, and gave him both the broad seal and signet to keep.

They several times pressed him to take the Covenant, but he never did, but followed his business so close, with such diligence and temper, that he was well beloved on all sides, and they reposed great trust in him. When he went out of Holland, he wrote to me to arm myself with patience in his absence, and likewise that I would not expect many letters as was his custom, for that was now impossible; but he hoped, that when we did meet again, it would be happy and of long continuance, and bade me trust God with him, as he did me, in whose mercy he hoped, being upon that duty he was obliged to, with a thousand kind expressions.

But God knows how great a surprise this me, being great with child, and two children with me not in the best condition to maintain them, and in daily fears of your father upon the private account of animosities amongst themselves in Scotland; but I did what I could to arm myself, and was kindly visited both by my relations and friends.

About this time my cousin Evelyn's wife [Footnote: Evelyn frequently mentions his "cousin Richard Fanshawe," in his Diary. On the 6th of February, 1651-2, he says, "I went to visit my cousin Richard Fanshawe, and divers other friends"; and on the 6th of March, in that year, he observes, "My cousin Richard Fanshawe came to visit me, and inform me of many considerable affairs." On the 23rd of November, 1654, he went to London to visit his "cousin Fanshawe."—Diary, vol. ii. pp. 48, 49, 98. Lady Brown, Mr. Evelyn's mother-in-law, died at Woodcot, in Kent, towards the end of October 1652.—Ibid. p. 61.] came to London, and had newly buried her mother, my Lady Brown, wife to Sir Richard Brown, that then was resident for the King at Paris. A little before she and I and Doctor Steward, a Clerk of the closet to King Charles the First, christened a daughter of Mr. Waters, near a year old. About this time, Lord Chief Justice Heath died at Calais, and several of the King's servants at Paris, amongst others Mr. Henry Murray, of his bedchamber, a very good man.

I now settled myself in a handsome lodging in London. With a heavy heart I stayed in this lodging almost seven months, and in that time I did not go abroad seven times, but spent my time in prayer to God for the deliverance of the King and my husband, whose danger was ever before my eyes. I was seldom without the best company, and sometimes my father would stay a week, for all had compassion on my condition. I removed to Queenstreet, and there in a very good lodging I was upon the 24th of June delivered of a daughter: in all this time I had but four letters from your father, which made the pain I was in more difficult to bear.

I went with my brother Fanshawe to Ware Park, and my sister went to Balls, to my father, both intending to meet in the winter; and so indeed we did with tears; for the 3rd of September following was fought the battle of Worcester, when the King being missed, and nothing heard of your father being dead or alive, for three days it was inexpressible what affliction I was in. I neither eat nor slept, but trembled at every motion I heard, expecting the fatal news, which at last came in their news-book, which mentioned your father a prisoner.

Then with some hopes I went to London, intending to leave my little girl Nan, the companion of my troubles, there, and so find out my husband wheresoever he was carried. But upon my coming to London, I met a messenger from him with a letter, which advised me of his condition, and told me he was very civilly used, and said little more, but that I should be in some room at Charing-cross, where he had promise from his keeper that he should rest there in my company at dinner-time: this was meant to him as a great favour. I expected him with impatience, and on the day appointed provided a dinner and room, as ordered, in which I was with my father and some of our friends, where, about eleven of the clock, we saw hundreds of poor soldiers, both English and Scotch, march all naked on foot, and many with your father, who was very cheerful in appearance, who after he had spoken and saluted me and his friends there, said, 'Pray let us not lose time, for I know not how little I have to spare. This is the chance of war; nothing venture, nothing have; so let us sit down and be merry whilst we may.' Then taking my hand in his and kissing me, 'Cease weeping, no other thing upon earth can move me: remember we are all at God's disposal.'

Then he began to tell how kind his Captain was to him, and the people as he passed offered him money, and brought him good things, and particularly Lady Denham, at Borstal-house, who would have given him all the money she had in her house, but he returned her thanks, and told her he had so ill kept his own, that he would not tempt his governor with more, but if she would give him a shirt or two, and some handkerchiefs, he would keep them as long as he could for her sake. She fetched him two smocks of her own, and some handkerchiefs, saying she was ashamed to give him them, but, having none of her sons at home, she desired him to wear them.

Thus we passed the time until order came to carry him to Whitehall, where, in a little room yet standing in the bowling-green, he was kept prisoner, without the speech of any, so far as they knew, ten weeks, and in expectation of death. They often examined him, and at last he grew so ill in health by the cold and hard marches he had undergone, and being pent up in a room close and small, that the scurvy brought him almost to death's door.

During the time of his imprisonment, I failed not constantly to go, when the clock struck four in the morning, with a dark lantern in my hand, all alone and on foot, from my lodging in Chancery Lane, at my cousin Young's, to Whitehall, in at the entry that went out of King Street into the bowling-green. There I would go under his window and softly call him: he, after the first time excepted, never failed to put out his head at the first call: thus we talked together, and sometimes I was so wet with the rain, that it went in at my neck and out at my heels. He directed me how I should make my addresses, which I did ever to their general, Cromwell, who had a great respect for your father, and would have bought him off to his service upon any terms.

Being one day to solicit for my husband's liberty for a time, he bade me bring the next day a certificate from a physician, that he was really ill. Immediately I went to Dr. Bathurst, that was by chance both physician to Cromwell and to our family, who gave me one very favourable in my husband's behalf. I delivered it at the Council Chamber, at three of the clock that afternoon, as he commanded me, and he himself moved, that seeing they could make no use of his imprisonment, whereby to lighten them in their business, he might have his liberty upon four thousand pounds bail, to take a course of physic, he being dangerously ill. Many spake against it, but most Sir Henry Vane, who said he would be as instrumental, for aught he knew, to hang them all that sat there, if ever he had opportunity, but if he had liberty for a time, that he might take the engagement before he went out: upon which Cromwell said, 'I never knew that the ENGAGEMENT [Footnote: Cromwell probably meant to pun upon this word.—In Ireland, "engagement" means an ISSUE; "an engagement in the neck," arm, &c., i.e., an issue in those places.] was a medicine for the scorbutic.' They, hearing their General say so, thought it obliged him, and so ordered him his liberty upon bail. His eldest brother, and sister Bedell, and self, were bound in four thousand pounds; and the latter end of November he came to my lodgings, at my cousin Young's. He there met many of his good friends and kindred; and my joy was inexpressible, and so was poor Nan's, of whom your poor father was very fond. I forgot to tell you, that when your father was taken prisoner of war, he, before they entered the house where he was, burned all his papers, which saved the lives and estates of many a brave gentleman.

When he came out of Scotland, he left behind him a box of writings, in which his patent of Baronet was, and his patent of additional arms, [Footnote: A coat of augmentation was granted to Richard Fanshawe, Esq., Remembrancer of the Exchequer, and to his family, by patent, dated at Jersey, 8th of February, 2 Car. II. 1650, being "Cheeky Argent and Azure, a Cross Gules." Grants of that kind to persons who distinguished themselves in the service of the King were very common, and consisted, in most cases, either of the lion of England, a fleur- de-lis, or, as in the instance of Mr. Fanshawe, of the Cross of St. George. Sir Richard was created a Baronet on the 2nd of September 1650.] which was safely sent after him, after the happy restoration of the King. You may read your father's demeanour of himself in this affair, wrote by his own hand, in a book by itself amongst your books, and it is a great masterpiece, as you will find.

Within ten days he fell very sick, and the fever settled in his throat and face so violently, that, for many days and nights, he slept no more but as he leaned on my shoulder as I walked: at last, after all the Doctor and Surgeon could do, it broke, and with that he had ease, and so recovered, God be praised! In 1652, he was advised to go to Bath for his scorbutic that still hung on him, but he deferred his journey until August, because I was delivered on the 30th of July of a daughter.

At his return, we went to live that winter following at Benfield, in Hertfordshire, a house of my niece Fanshawe's. In this winter my husband went to wait on his good friend the Earl of Strafford, in Yorkshire; and there my Lord offered him a house of his in Tankersly Park, which he took, and paid 120 l. a year for. When my husband returned, we prepared to go in the spring to this place, but were so confined, that my husband could not stir five miles from home without leave. About February following, my brother Neuce died, at his house at Much Hadham, in Hertfordshire. My sister, Margaret Harrison, desired to go to London, and there we left her: she soon after married Mr. Edmund Turner, afterwards Sir Edmund.

In March we with our three children, Anne, Richard, and Betty, went into Yorkshire, where we lived a harmless country life, minding only the country sports and country affairs. Here my husband translated Luis de Camoens; and on October 8th, 1653, I was delivered of my daughter Margaret. I found all the neighbourhood very civil and kind upon all occasions; the place plentiful and healthful, and very pleasant, but there was no fruit: we planted some, and my Lord Strafford says now, that what we planted is the best fruit in the North.

The house of Tankersly and Park are both very pleasant and good, and we lived there with great content; but God had ordered it should not last, for upon the 20th of July 1654, at three o'clock in the afternoon, died our most dearly beloved daughter Ann, whose beauty and wit exceeded all that ever I saw of her age. She was between nine and ten years old, very tall, and the dear companion of my travels and sorrows. She lay sick but five days of the smallpox, in which time she expressed so many wise and devout sayings, as is a miracle for her years. We both wished to have gone into the same grave with her. She lies buried in Tankersly church, and her death made us both desirous to quit that fatal place to us; and so the week after her death we did, and came to Hamerton, and were half a year with my sister Bedell. Then my husband was sent for to London, there to stay, by command of the High Court of Justice, and not to go five miles from that town, but to appear once a month before them. We then went again to my cousin Young's, in Chancery Lane: and about Christmas my husband got leave to go to Frog-Pool, in Kent, to my brother Warwick's; where, upon the 22nd of February 1655, I was delivered of a daughter, whom we named Ann, to keep in remembrance her dear sister, whom we had newly lost. We returned to our lodgings in Chancery Lane, where my husband was forced to attend till Christmas 1655; and then we went down to Jenkins, to Sir Thomas Fanshawe's; but upon New Year's Day my husband fell very sick, and the scorbutic again prevailed, so much that it drew his upper lip awry, upon which we that day came to London, into Chancery Lane, but not to my cousin Young's, but to a house we took of Sir George Carey, for a year. There by the advice of Doctor Bathurst and Doctor Ridgley, my husband took physic for two months together, and at last, God be praised! he perfectly recovered his sickness, and his lip was as well as ever.

In this house, upon the 12th day of July in 1656, I was delivered of a daughter, named Mary; and in this month died my second daughter, Elizabeth, that I had left with my sister Boteler, at Frog-Pool, to see if that air would recover her; but she died of a hectic fever, and lies buried in the church of Foots Cray. My husband, weary of the town, and being advised to go into the country for his health, procured leave to go in September to Bengy, in Hertford, to a little house lent us by my brother Fanshawe.

It happened at that time there was a very ill kind of fever, of which many died, and it ran generally through all families: this we and all our family fell sick of, and my husband's and mine after some months turned to quartan agues; but I being with child, none thought I could live, for I was brought to bed of a son in November,[Footnote: "This son, Henry, lies buried in Bengy church."] ten weeks before my time; and thence forward until April 1658, I had two fits every day, that brought me so low that I was like an anatomy. I never stirred out of my bed seven months, nor during that time eat flesh, nor fish, nor bread, but sage posset drink, and pancake or eggs, or now and then a turnip or carrot. Your father was likewise very ill, but he rose out of his bed some hours daily, and had such a greediness upon him, that he would eat and drink more than ordinary persons that eat most, though he could not stand upright without being held, and in perpetual sweats, and that so violent that it ran down day and night like water. This I have told you that you may see how near dying we were; for which recovery I humbly praise God. He got leave in August to go to Bath, which, God be praised! perfectly recovered us, and so we returned into Hertfordshire, to the Friary of Ware, which we hired of Mrs. Heydon for a year. This place we accounted happy to us, because in October we heard the news of Cromwell's death, upon which my husband began to hope that he should get loose of his fetters, in which he had been seven years; and going to London, in company with my Lord Philip, Earl of Pembroke, he lamented his case of his bonds to him that was his old and constant friend. He told him that if he would dine with him the next day, he would give him some account of that business. The next day he said to him, 'Mr. Fanshawe, I must send my eldest son into France; if you will not take it ill that I desire your company with him and care of him for one year, I will procure you your bonds within this week.' My husband was overjoyed to get loose upon any terms that were innocent, so, having seen his bonds cancelled, he went into France to Paris, from whence he by letter gave an account to Lord Chancellor Clarendon of his being got loose, and desired him to acquaint his Majesty of it, and to send him his commands, which was about April 1659. He did to this effect, that his Majesty was then going a journey, which afterwards proved to Spain; but upon his return, which would be about the beginning of winter, my husband should come to him, and that he should have, in present, the place of one of the Masters of Request, and the Secretary of the Latin Tongue. Then my husband sent me word of this, and bade me bring my son Richard, and my eldest daughters with me to Paris, for that he intended to put them to a very good school that he had found at Paris. We went as soon as I could possibly accommodate myself with money and other necessaries, with my three children, one maid, and one man. I could not go without a pass, and to that purpose I went to my cousin Henry Nevill, [Footnote: He was her cousin, being the second son of Sir Harry Nevill the younger, of Billingbere, in Essex, by Elizabeth, daughter of Sir John Smythe, of Ostenhanger, sister to the first Viscount Strangford.] one of the High Court of Justice, where he was then sitting at Whitehall. I told him my husband had sent for me and his son, to place him there, and that he desired his kindness to help me to a pass: he went in to the then masters, and returned to me, saying, 'that by a trick my husband had got his liberty, but for me and his children, upon no conditions we should not stir.' I made no reply, but thanked my cousin, Henry Nevill, and took my leave. I sat me down in the next room, full sadly to consider what I should do, desiring God to help me in so just a cause as I then was in. I began and thought if I were denied a passage then, they would ever after be more severe on all occasions, and it might be very ill for us both. I was ready to go, if I had a pass, the next tide, and might be there before they could suspect I was gone: these thoughts put this invention in my head.

At Wallingford House, the Office was kept where they gave passes: thither I went in as plain a way and speech as I could devise, leaving my maid at the gate, who was much a finer gentlewoman than myself. With as ill mien and tone as I could express, I told a fellow I found in the Office that I desired a pass for Paris, to go to my husband. 'Woman, what is your husband, and your name?' 'Sir,' said I, with many courtesies, 'he is a young merchant, and my name is Ann Harrison.' 'Well,' said he, 'it will cost you a crown.'—said I, 'That is a great sum for me, but pray put in a man, my maid, and three children.' All which he immediately did, telling me a malignant would give him five pounds for such a pass.

I thanked him kindly, and so went immediately to my lodgings; and with my pen I made the great H of Harrison, two ff, and the rrs, an n, and the i, an s, and the s, an h, and the o, an a, and the n, a w, so completely, that none could find out the change. With all speed I hired a barge, and that night at six o'clock I went to Gravesend, and from thence by coach to Dover, where, upon my arrival, the searchers came and demanded my pass, which they were to keep for their discharge. When they had read it, they said, 'Madam, you may go when you please;' but says one, 'I little thought they would give a pass to so great a malignant, especially in so troublesome a time as this.'

About nine o'clock at night I went on board the packet-boat, and about eight o'clock in the morning landed safe, God be praised! at Calais. I went to Mr. Booth's, an English merchant, and a very honest man. There I rested two days; but upon the next day he had advice from Dover, that a post was sent to stay me from London, because they had sent for me to my lodgings by a messenger of the Court, to know why, and upon what business, I went to France. Then I discovered to him my invention of the changing my name, at which as at their disappointment we all laughed, and so did your father, and as many as knew the deceit. We hired a waggon-coach, for there is no other at Calais, and began our journey about the beginning of June 1659.

Coming one night to Abbeville, the Governor sent his Lieutenant to me, to let me know my husband was well the week before, that he had seen him at Paris, and had promised him to take care of me in my going through his government, there being much robbery daily committing; that he would advise me take care of the garrison soldiers, and giving them a pistole a piece, they would convey me very safely. This, he said, the Governor would have told me himself, but that he was in bed with the gout; I thanked him, and accepted his proffer. The next morning he sent me ten troopers well armed, and when I had gone about four leagues, as we ascended a hill, says some of these, 'Madam, look out, but fear nothing.' They rid all up to a well-mounted troop of horse, about fifty or more, which, after some parley, wheeled about into the woods again. When we came upon the hill, I asked how it was possible so many men so well armed should turn, having so few to oppose them; at which they laughed, and said, 'Madam, we are all of a company, and quarter in this town. The truth is, our pay is short, and we are forced to keep ourselves this way; but we have this rule, that if we in a party guard any company, the rest never molest them, but let them pass free.'

I having passed all danger, as they said, gave them a pistole each man, and so left them and went on my journey, and met my husband at St. Dennis, God be praised! The 20th day of October, my then only son died of the small-pox; he lies buried in the Protestant Church, near Paris, between the Earl of Bristol and Doctor Steward. Both my eldest daughters had the small-pox at the same time, and though I neglected them, and day and night attended my dear son, yet it pleased God they recovered and he died, the grief of which made me miscarry, and caused a sickness of three weeks.

After this, in the beginnings of November, the King came to visit his mother, who was at her own house at Combes, two leagues from Paris, and thither went my husband and myself. I had not seen him in almost twelve years: he told me that if it pleased God to restore him to his kingdoms, my husband should partake of his happiness in as great a share as any servants he had. Then he asked me many questions of England, and fell into discourse with my husband privately two hours, and then commanded him to follow him to Flanders. His Majesty went the next day, my husband that day month, which was the beginning of December. I went with our family to Calais, and my husband sent me privately to London for money in January. I returned him one hundred and fifty pounds, with which he went to the King, and I followed to Newport, Bruges, and Ghent, and to Brussels, where the King received us very graciously, with the Princess Royal and the Dukes of York and Gloucester. After staying three weeks at Brussels, we went to Breda, where we heard the happy news of the King's return to England. In the beginning of May we went with all the Court to the Hague, where I first saw the Queen of Bohemia, who was exceeding kind to all of us. Here the King and all the Royal Family were entertained at a very great supper by the States; and now business of state took up much time.

The King promised my husband he should be one of the Secretaries of State, and both the now Duke of Ormond, and the Lord Chancellor Clarendon, were witnesses of it, yet that false man made the King break his word for his own accommodation, and placed Mr. Norris, a poor country gentleman of about two hundred pounds a year, a fierce

Presbyterian, and one that never saw the King's face: but still promises were made of the reversion to your father.

Upon the King's restoration, the Duke of York, then made Admiral, appointed ships to carry over the company and servants of the King, who were very great. His Highness appointed for my husband and his family a third-rate frigate, called the Speedwell; but his Majesty commanded my husband to wait on him in his own ship. We had by the States' order sent on board to the King's most eminent servants, great store of provisions: for our family we had sent on board the Speedwell a tierce of claret, a hogshead of Rhenish wine, six dozen of fowls, a dozen of gammons of bacon, a great basket of bread, and six sheep, two dozen of neats' tongues, and a great box of sweetmeats. Thus taking our leaves of those obliging persons we had conversed with in the Hague, we went on board upon the 23rd of May, about two o'clock in the afternoon. The King embarked at four of the clock, upon which we set sail, the shore being covered with people, and shouts from all places of a good voyage, which was seconded with many volleys of shot interchanged: so favourable was the wind, that the ships' wherries went from ship to ship to visit their friends all night long. But who can sufficiently express the joy and gallantry of that voyage, to see so many great ships, the best in the world, to hear the trumpets and all other music, to see near a hundred brave ships sail before the wind with vast cloths and streamers, the neatness and cleanness of the ships, the strength and jollity of the mariners, the gallantry of the commanders, the vast plenty of all sorts of provisions; but above all, the glorious majesties of the King and his two brothers, were so beyond man's expectation and expression! The sea was calm, the moon shone at full, and the sun suffered not a cloud to hinder his prospect of the best sight, by whose light, and the merciful bounty of God, he was set safely on shore at Dover in Kent, upon the 25th [Footnote: Probably a mistake for the 26th] of May, 1660.

So great were the acclamations and numbers of people, that it reached like one street from Dover to Whitehall: we lay that night at Dover, and the next day we went in Sir Arnold Braem's [Footnote: Of a Dutch family settled at Bridge, in Kent. The house at Dover, in which Lady Fanshawe lay, was built by Jacob Braem, and is, or was in Hasted's time, the Custom-house. The family is now extinct.] coach towards London, where on Sunday night we came to a house in the Savoy. My niece, Fanshawe, then lay in the Strand, where I stood to see the King's entry with his brothers; surely the most pompous show that ever was, for the hearts of all men in this kingdom moved at his will.

The next day I went with other ladies of the family to congratulate his Majesty's happy arrival, who received me with great grace, and promised me future favours to my husband and self. His Majesty gave my husband his picture, set with small diamonds, when he was a child: it is a great rarity, because there never was but one. We took a house in Portugal Row, Lincoln's-inn Fields. My husband had not long entered upon his office, but he found an oppression from Secretary Nicholas, to his great vexation, for he, as much as in him lay, engrossed all the petitions, which really, by the foundation, belonged to the Master of the Requests; and in this he was countenanced by Lord Chancellor Clarendon, his great patron, notwithstanding he had married Sir Thomas Aylesbury's daughter, that was one of the Masters of the Requests.

This year I sent for my daughter Nan from my sister Boteler's, in Kent, where I had left her; and my daughter Mary died in Hertfordshire in August, and lies buried in Hertford church, in my father's vault.

In the latter end of the summer I miscarried, when I was near half gone with child, of three sons, two hours one after the other. I think it was with the hurry of business I then was in, and perpetual company that resorted to us of all qualities, some for kindness and some for their own advantage.

As that was a time of advantage, so it was of great expense, for on April the 23rd, 1661, the King was crowned, when my husband, being in waiting, rode upon his Majesty's left hand [Footnote: Evelyn says, that at the coronation of Charles the Second were "Two persons, representing the Dukes of Normandy and Aquitaine, viz., Sir Richard Fanshawe and Sir Herbert Price, in fantastic habits."-Diary, vol. ii. p. 168.] with very rich footcloths, and four men in very rich liveries; and this year we furnished our house and paid all our debts which we had contracted during the war.

The 8th day of May following, the King rode to the Parliament, and then my husband rode in the same manner. His Majesty had commanded my husband to execute the place of the Chancellor of the Garter, both because he understood it better than any, and was to have the reversion of it. The first feast of St. George, my husband was proxy for the Earl of Bristol, and was installed for him Knight of the Garter. The Duke of Buckingham put on his robes, and the Duke of Ormond his spurs, in the stall of the Earl of Bristol.

Now it was the business of the Chancellor to put your father as far from the King as he could, because his ignorance in state affairs was daily discovered by your father, who showed it to the King; but at that time the King was so content that he should almost and alone manage his affairs, that he might have more time for his pleasure, that his faults were not so visible as otherwise they would have been, and afterwards proved. But now he sends to your father and tells him that he was, by the King's particular choice, resolved on to be sent to Lisbon with the King's letter and picture to the Princess, now our Queen, which then, indeed, was an employment any nobleman would be glad of; but the design from that time forth was to fix him here.

When your father was gone on this errand, I stayed in our house in Portugal Row, and at Christmas I received the New Year's gifts belonging to his places, which is the custom, of two tuns of wine at the Custom-house, for Master of Requests, and fifteen ounces of gilt plate at the Jewel-house, as Secretary of the Latin Tongue.

At the latter end of Christmas my husband returned from Lisbon, and was very well received by the King; and upon the 22nd of February following I was delivered of my daughter Elizabeth.

Upon the 8th of June,|Footnote: Query, 8th| 1662, my husband was made a Privy Councillor of Ireland; and some time after my Lord and Lady Ormond went into Ireland, and upon my taking leave of her Grace, she gave me a turquoise and diamond bracelet, and my husband a fasset |Footnote: A diamond cut into facets; a brilliant.| diamond ring. I never parted from her upon a journey but she ever gave me some present. When her daughter, the Lady Mary Cavendish, was married, none were present but his grandmother and father, and my husband and self; they were married in my Lord Duke's lodging in Whitehall, and given by the King, who came privately without any train. |Footnote: According to Collins' Peerage, Mary, second daughter of James Duke of Ormond, married William Cavendish, ninth Duke of Devonshire, at Kilkenny in Ireland, on the 27th of October, 1662. Lady Fanshawe's statement proves that he was mistaken.|

As soon as the King had notice of the Queen's landing, he immediately sent my husband that night to welcome her Majesty on shore, and followed himself the next day; and upon the 21st of May the King married the Queen at Portsmouth, in the presence-chamber of his Majesty's house.

There was a rail across the upper part of the room, in which entered only the King and Queen, the Bishop of London, the Marquis de Sande, the Portuguese Ambassador, and my husband: in the other part of the room there were many of the nobility and servants to their Majesties. The Bishop of London declared them married in the name of the Father, and of the Son, and of the Holy Ghost; and then they caused the ribbons her Majesty wore to be cut in little pieces, and, as far as they would go, every one had some.|Footnote: As it must be inferred that Lady Fanshawe derived her information from her husband, who, she says, was present, her account of the ceremony is deserving of attention, because some doubts have been entertained as to the manner in which it was solemnised.-See Bishop Kennett's Historical Register, p. 693.|

Upon the 29th of May their Majesties came to Hampton Court, where was all that pretended to her Majesty's service, and all the King's servants, ladies and other persons of quality, who received her Majesty in several rooms, according to their several qualifications.

The next morning, about eleven o'clock, the Duchess of Ormond and her daughter, the now Lady Cavendish, and myself, went to wait on her Majesty as soon as her Majesty was dressed; where I had the honour from the King, who was then present, to tell the Queen who I was, saying many kind things of me to ingratiate me with her Majesty, whereupon her Majesty gave her hand to me to kiss, with promises of her future favour. After this we remained in Hampton Court, in the Requests' lodgings, my husband being then

41

in waiting until the 10th day of August, upon which day he received his despatches for Ambassador to Portugal.

His Majesty was graciously pleased to promise my husband his picture, which afterwards we received, set with diamonds, to the value of three or four hundred pounds, his Majesty having been pleased to give my husband, at his first going to Portugal, his picture at length, in his garter-robes: my husband had also by his Majesty's order, out of the wardrobe, a crimson velvet cloth of state, fringed and laced with gold, with a chair, a footstool, and cushions, and two other stools of the same, with a Persian carpet to lay under them, and a suit of fine tapestry hanging for that room, with two velvet altar-cloths for the chapel, and fringed with gold, with surplices, altar cloths, and napkins, of fine linen, with a Bible, in Ogleby's print and cuts, two Common Prayer-books, in folio and quarto, with eight hundred ounces of gilt plate, and four thousand ounces of white plate; but there wanted a velvet bed, which he should have had by custom.

Thus having perfected the ceremonies of taking leave of their Majesties, and receiving their commands, and likewise taking our leaves of our friends, as I said, upon Sunday the 10th of August we took our journey to Portugal [Footnote: Evelyn says, "5th of August 1662, to London, and next day to Hampton Court, and took leave of Sir R. Fanshawe, now going Ambassador to Portugal."—Diary, vol. ii. p. 195.] carrying our three daughters with us, Katherine, Margaret, and Ann.

This night we lay at Windsor, where, on Monday the 11th, in the morning, we went to prayers to the King's Chapel with Doctor Heavers, my husband's Chaplain. On our return we were visited by the Provost of Eton, and divers others of the clergy of that place, and Sir Thomas Woodcock, the chief commander of that place, in the absence of Lord Mordaunt, Lord Constable of Windsor Castle.

Upon the desire of some there, my husband left some of his coats-of- arms, which he carried with him for that purpose, as the custom of ambassadors is, to dispose of where they lodge.[Footnote: This custom is still retained in the instances of the Lords Lieutenant of Ireland.]

That night we lay at Bagshot; Tuesday the 12th, we dined at Basingstoke, and lay at Andover; Wednesday the 13th, we dined at Salisbury, and there lay that night, and borrowed in the afternoon the Dean of Westminster's coach, being willing to ease all our own horses for half a day, having a long journey to go.

We went in the Dean's coach to see Wilton, being but two miles from Salisbury. We found Lord Herbert at home; he entertained us with great civility and kindness, and gave my husband a very fine greyhound bitch: his father, the Earl of Pembroke, being then at London. We visited the famous church, and at our return to our lodgings, were visited by the Right Reverend Father in God, Doctor Henchman, the Bishop of that place, and Doctor Holles, the Dean of that place, and Doctor Earle, Dean of Westminster, since, by the former Bishop's remove to the See of London, now Bishop of Salisbury.

On Thursday the 14th, my husband and I, with our children, having begged of the Bishop his blessing at his own house, dined at Blandford, in Dorsetshire. Sir William Portman hath a very fine seat within a mile of it. We lodged that night at Dorchester: on Friday the 15th we lay at Axminster, and Saturday the 16th at Exeter, and went to prayers at the Cathedral church, accompanied by the principal divines of that place. On Sunday the 17th, we stayed all that day, and on Monday the 18th, we lay at a very ill lodging, of which I have forgotten the name; and on Tuesday the 19th, we went to Plymouth, where, within six miles of the town, we were met by some of the chief merchants of that place, and of the chief officers of that garrison, who all accompanied us to the house of one Mr. Tyler, a merchant.

Upon our arrival, the Governor of that garrison, one Sir John Skelton, visited us, and did us the favour to keep us company, with many of his officers, during our stay in that town. Sir John Hele, as soon as he heard of our being there, sent my husband a fat buck; and my cousin Edgcombe, of Mount Edgcombe, a mile from Plymouth, sent him another buck, and came, as soon as he heard we were there, from a house of his twelve miles from Mount Edgcombe, to which he came only to keep us company. From whence, the next day after his arrival, he with his Lady, and Sir Richard Edgcombe, his eldest son, and others of his children, came to visit us at Plymouth; and the day after we dined at Mount Edgcombe, where we were very nobly treated. At our coming home, they would need accompany us over the river to our lodgings. The next day the Mayor and Aldermen came to visit my husband; and the next day we had a great feast at Mr. Seale's house, the father of our landlord. Our being so well lodged and treated by the inhabitants of this town was upon my father's score, whose deputies some of them were, he being one of the Farmers of the Custom-house to receive the King's customs of that port.

On Sunday the 30th, the wind coming fair, we embarked, accompanied by my cousin Edgcombe and all his family, and with much company of the town, that would show their kindness until the last. Taking our leave of our landlord and landlady, we gave her twenty pieces of gold to buy her a ring, and they presented my children with many pretty toys. Thus, on Monday, at nine o'clock in the morning we were received on board the Ruby frigate, commanded by Captain Robinson. We had very many presents sent us on board by divers gentlemen, among which my cousin Edgcombe sent us a brace of fat bucks, three milk goats, wine, ale and beer, with fruit of several sorts, biscuit and sweetmeats.

On Monday the 31st of August 1662, we set sail for Lisbon, and landed the 14th of September, our style, between the Conde de St. Laurence's house and Belem, God be praised! all in good health. As soon as we had anchored, the English Consul, with the merchants, came on board us; but we went presently to a house of the Duke of Aveiros, where my husband was placed by his Majesty when he was there before, in which he had then left his chief Secretary and one other, with some others of his family. The first that visited incognito there, for he was not to own any till he had made his entry, was the King of Portugal's Secretary, Antonio de Sousa: there came about that time also the Earl of Inchiquin, and Count Schomberg, to visit us. The 28/18th day, my husband went privately on board the frigate, in which he came with all his family; to whom the King sent a nobleman to receive him on shore, with his own and Queen-mother's, and very many coaches of the nobility. As soon as they met, there passed great salutations of cannons from the ships to the frigate in which my husband came, and from our ships to the King's forts, and from all the forts innumerable shots returned again.

So soon as my husband landed, he entered the King's coach, and the nobleman that fetched him, whose name I have forgot. Before him went the English Consul, with all the merchants; on his right hand went four pages; on the left side the coach, by the horses' heads, eight footmen all clothed in rich livery; in the coach that followed went my husband's own gentlemen, after the coach of state empty, and those that did him the favour to accompany him: thus they went to the house where my husband lodged. The King entertained him with great plenty of provisions in all kinds, three suppers and three dinners, and all manner of utensils belonging thereunto, as the custom of that country is.

Their Majesties did for some time furnish the house, till my husband could otherwise provide himself in town. The Abadessa of the Alcantara, niece to the Queen-mother, natural daughter of the Duke of Medina Sidonia, sent to welcome me into the country a very noble present of perfumes, waters, and sweetmeats; and during my abode at Lisbon we often made visits and interchanged messages, to my great content, for she was a very fine lady. On the 19/29th, one Mr. Bridgewood, a merchant, sent me a silver basin and ewers for a present.

On the 10th of October, stilo novo, my husband had his audience of his Majesty in his palace, at Lisbon; going in the King's coach with the same nobleman and in the same form as he made his entry. The King received him with great kindness and respect, much to his satisfaction. On the 11th, Don Joam de Sousa, the Queen's Vidor, came from her Majesty to us both to welcome us into the country. On the 13th, her Majesty sent her chief coach, accompanied by other coaches, to fetch my husband to the audience of her Majesty, where she received him very graciously; and the same day he had audience of Don Pedro, the King's brother, at his own palace. Saturday, the 14th, her Majesty sent her best coach for me and my children. When we came there, the Captain of the Guard received me at the foot of the stairs; all my people going before me, as the custom is. On each side were the guards placed, with halberds in their hands, as far as the presence-chamber door. There I was received by the Queen's Lord Chamberlain, who carried me to the door of the next room, where the Queen was. Then the Queen's principal lady, as our groom of the stole, received me, telling me she had command from the Queen to bid me welcome to that Court, from the ships to the frigate in which my husband came, and from our ships to the King's forts, and from all the forts innumerable shots returned again.

So soon as my husband landed, he entered the King's coach, and the nobleman that fetched him, whose name I have forgot. Before him went the English Consul, with all the merchants; on his right hand went four pages; on the left side the coach, by the horses' heads, eight footmen all clothed in rich livery; in the coach that followed went my husband's own gentlemen, after the coach of state empty, and those that did him the favour to accompany him: thus they went to the house where my husband lodged. The King entertained him with great plenty of provisions in all kinds, three suppers and three dinners, and all manner of utensils belonging thereunto, as the custom of that country is.

Their Majesties did for some time furnish the house, till my 'husband could otherwise provide himself in town. The Abadessa of the Alcantara, niece to the Queen-mother, natural daughter of the Duke of Medina Sidonia, sent to welcome me into the country a very noble present of perfumes, waters, and sweetmeats; and during my abode at Lisbon we often made visits and interchanged messages, to my great content, for she was a very fine lady. On the 19/29th, one Mr. Bridgewood, a merchant, sent me a silver basin and ewers for a present.

On the 10th of October, stilo novo, my husband had his audience of his Majesty in his palace, at Lisbon; going in the King's coach with the same nobleman and in the same form as he made his entry. The King received him with great kindness and respect, much to his satisfaction. On the nth, Don Joam de Sousa, the Queen's Vidor, came from her Majesty to us both to welcome us into the country. On the 13th, her Majesty sent her chief coach, accompanied by other coaches, to fetch my husband to the audience of her Majesty, where she received him very graciously; and the same day he had audience of Don Pedro, the King's brother, at his own palace. Saturday, the 14th, her Majesty sent her best coach for me and my children. When we came there, the Captain of the Guard received me at the foot of the stairs; all my people going before me, as the custom is. On each side were the guards placed, with halberds in their hands, as far as the presence-chamber door. There I was received by the Queen's Lord Chamberlain, who carried me to the door of the next room, where the Queen was. Then the Queen's principal lady, as our groom of the stole, received me, telling me she had command from the Queen to bid me welcome to that Court, and to accompany me to her Majesty's presence. She sat in the next room, which was very large, in a black velvet chair, with arms, upon a black velvet carpet, with a state of the same. She had caused a low chair, without arms, to be set at some distance from her, about two yards on her left hand, on which side stood all the noblemen; on her right, all the ladies of the Court.

After making my reverences due to her Majesty, according to custom, and said those respects which became me to her Majesty, she sat down; and when I presented my daughters to her, she having expressed much grace and favour to me and mine, bade me sit down, which at first I refused, desiring to wait on her Majesty, as my Queen's mother; but she pressing me again, I sat down; and then she made her discourse of England, and asked questions of the Queen's health and liking of our country, with some little hints of her own and her family's condition, which having continued better than half an hour, I took my leave. During my stay at Court I several times waited on the Queen-Mother; truly she was a very honourable, wise woman, and I believe had been very handsome. She was magnificent in her discourse and nature, but in the prudentest manner; she was ambitious, but not vain; she loved government, and I do believe the quitting of it did shorten her life.

After saluting the ladies and noblemen of the Court, I went home as I came. The next day the Secretary of State and his Lady came to visit me: she had, at my arrival, sent me a present of sweetmeats. My husband had left in this person's family one of his pages to improve himself in writing and reading the Spanish tongue, until his return again to that Court, when he went the last year to England, in consideration of which we presented his Lady with a piece of India plate, of about two hundred pounds sterling. They were both very civil, worthy persons, and had formerly been in England, where the King, Charles the First, had made his son an English Baron.|Footnote: No record is known to exist of any foreigner having been created a Peer by Charles the First: nor does it appear likely from the names of

44

persons created Baronets by Charles the First, that Lady Fanshawe could mean Baronet. The splendid and elaborate work entitled the "Memorias Genealogicas da Casa de Sousa," does not advert to the circumstance.] She told me in discourse one day this of a French Ambassador, that had lately been in that Court, and lodged next to her:—

There was a numerous sort of people about the Ambassador's door, as is usual amongst them. A poor little boy, that his mother had animated daily to cry for relief so troublesomely, that at last the Ambassador would say, 'What noise is that at the gate of perpetual screaming? I will have it so no more:' upon which they carried the child to his mother, and bade her keep him at home, for it screamed like a devil, and if it returned, the porter swore he would punish him severely. Not many days after, according to his former custom, the child returned, louder than before, if possible; the porter keeping his word, took the boy and pulled off his rags, and anointed him all over with honey, leaving no part undone, and very thick, and then threw him into a tub of fine feathers, which as soon as he had done, he set him on his legs and frightened him home to his mother, who seeing this thing, for none living could guess him a boy, ran out into the city, the child squeaking after her, and all the people in the streets after them, thinking it was a devil or some strange creature.

But to return to the business: we were visited by many persons of the Court, some upon business, and others upon compliment, which is more formal than pleasant, for they are not generally a cheerful people. About February the King intended to go into the field and lead his army himself: during this resolution my husband prepared himself to wait on his Majesty, which cost him much, these kind of expenses in that place being scarce and very dear; but the Council would not suffer him to go, and so that ended. The King loved hunting much, and ever when he went would send my husband some of what he killed, which was stag and wild boar, both excellent meat. We kept the Queen's birthday with great feasting: we had all the English merchants.

There was, during my stay in this town, a Portugal merchant jealous of his mistress favouring an Englishman, whom he entertained with much kindness, hiding his suspicion. One evening he invited him to see a country-house and eat a collation, which he did; after which the merchant, with three or four more of his friends, for a rarity showed him a cave hard by the house, which went in at a very narrow hole, but within was very capacious, in the side of a high mountain. It was so dark that they carried a torch. Says one to the Englishman, 'Did you ever know where bats dwell?' he replied no; 'Then here, Sir,' say they, 'you shall see them;' then, holding up the light to the roof, they saw millions hanging by their legs. So soon as they had done, they, frightening the birds, made them all fly about them, and putting out the light ran away, and left the Englishman there to get out as well as he could, which was not until the next morning.

This winter I fell sick of an aguish distemper, being then with child; but I believe it was with eating more grapes than I am accustomed to, being tempted by their goodness, especially the Frontiniac, which exceed all I ever eat in Spain and France.

The beginning of May 1663, there happened in Lisbon an insurrection of the people of the town, about a suspicion, as they pretended, of some persons disaffected to the public; upon which they plundered the Archbishop's house, and the Marquis of Marialva's house, and broke into the treasury; but after about ten thousand of these ordinary people had run for six or seven hours about the town, crying 'Kill all that is for the Castile,' they were appeased by their Priests, who carried the Sacrament amongst them, threatening excommunication, which, with the night, made them depart with their plunder. Some few persons were lost, but not many.

Upon the 10th of June came news to this Court of the total rout of Don John of Austria at the battle of Evora;[Footnote: Pepys, speaking of this battle, in which the Portuguese completely defeated the Spaniards, says—"4th July, 1663. Sir Allen Apsley showed the Duke the Lisbon Gazette, in Spanish, where the late victory is set down particularly, and to the great honour of the English beyond measure. They have since taken back Evora, which was lost to the Spaniards, the English making the assault, and lost not more than three men."-Diary, vol. ii-p. 68.] after which our house and tables were full of distressed, honest, brave English soldiers, who by their own and their fellows' valour had got one of the greatest victories that ever was.

These poor but brave men were almost lost between the Portuguese poverty and the Lord Chancellor Hyde's neglect, not to give it a worse name.[Footnote: It appears however, from Sir Robert Southwell's Account of Portugal (p.138), that Charles II was so pleased with the gallantry of his troops at the battle of Evora, (or, as it is more commonly called by historians, of Ameixal,) that he caused a gratuity of 40,000 crowns to be distributed among them. It would seem that the "neglect" of which Lady Fanshawe complains, was entirely on the side of the Portuguese. Sir Robert Southwell mentions some curious anecdotes on this subject, particularly with reference to the statement in the Lisbon Gazette, alluded to in the preceding note.] While my husband stayed there, he did what he could, but not proportionably either to their merits or wants.

About this time my husband sent great assistance to the Governor of Tangiers, the Earl of Peterborough then being Governor, whose letters of supplication and thanks for kindness and care, my husband and I have yet to show.

June the 26th, I was delivered of a son ten weeks before my time: he lived some hours, and was christened Richard by our Chaplain, Mr. Marsden, who performed the ceremony of the Church of England at his burial, and then laid him in the Parish Church in which we lived, in the principal part of the chancel.

The Queen sent to condole with me for the loss of my son, and the Marquees de Castel Melhor, the Marquees de Nica, the Condessa de Villa Franca, (Donna Maria e Antonia,) with many other ladies, and several good gentlewomen that were English merchants' wives.

Several times we saw the Feasts of Bulls, and at them had great voiders of dried sweetmeats brought us upon the King's account, with rich drinks.

Once we had some dispute about some English Commanders that thought themselves not well enough placed at the show, according to their merit, by the King's officers, which did so ill represent it to my husband that he was extremely concerned at it. Upon notice being given to the Chief Minister, the Conde de Castel Melhor came from the King to my husband, after having examined the business, and desired that there might be no misunderstanding between the King and him, that the business was only the impertinence of a servant, and that it might so pass. My husband was well satisfied, and presented his most humble acknowledgments to the King for his care and favour to him, as well as the honour he had received. The Conde de Castel Melhor, when he had finished his visit to my husband, came to my apartment, and told me he hoped I took no offence at what had passed at the feast, because the King had heard I was sad to see my husband troubled; assuring me that his Majesty and the whole Court desired nothing more than that we should receive all content imaginable. I gave him many thanks for the honour of his visit, and desired him to present my humble service to the King, assuring him, that my husband and I had all the respect imaginable for his Majesty; true it was, according to the English fashion, I did make a little whine when I saw my husband disordered, but I should ever remain his Majesty's humble servant, with my most humble thanks to his Excellency. And so he returned well satisfied.

The 14th, the Chief Ministers met my husband in order to his return home for England, and expressed a great trouble to part from him; they from the King presented my husband with twelve thousand crowns in gold plate, with many compliments and favours from the King, whom my husband waited on the next day to receive his Majesty's commands for his Master in England. After giving his Majesty many thanks for the many honours he had received from his Majesty's kind acceptance of his service, he thanked his Majesty for his present, saying that he wished his Majesty's bounteous kindness to him might not prejudice his Majesty, in this example, by the next coming ambassador; to which his Majesty replied, 'I am sure it cannot, for I shall never have such another ambassador.' Then my husband took his leave, performing all those ceremonies with the same persons and coaches as he made at his entry.

Upon the 19th of August my husband and I took our leaves of the Queen- Mother, at her house, who had commanded all her ladies to give attendance, though her Majesty was then in a retired condition.

Her Majesty expressed much resentment at our leaving the Court; and after our respects paid to her Majesty, and I receiving her Majesty's commands to our Queen, with a present, I took my leave with the same ceremony of coaches and persons as I had waited on her Majesty twice before.

Upon the 20th, my husband took his leave of Don Pedro, his Majesty's brother. The 21st of August, the Secretary of State came to visit me from the King and Queen, wishing me a prosperous voyage, and presented me with a very noble present. The same day I took my leave of my good neighbour the Condessa de Palma, as I had done of all the ladies of my acquaintance before, who all presented me with fine presents, as did my good neighbour the Countess Santa Graca, who had with her, when I went to take my leave, many persons of quality, that came on purpose there to take their leaves of me, and from whom I received great civility, and the Countess gave me a very great banquet.

On the 23rd of August 1663, we, accompanied by many persons of all sorts, went on board the King of England's frigate, called the Reserve, commanded by Captain Holmes, where, as soon as I was on board, the Conde de Castel Melhor sent me a very great and noble present, a part of which was the finest case of waters that ever I saw, being made of Brazil wood, garnished with silver, the bottles of crystal, garnished with the same, and filled with rich amber-water.

Lisbon with the river is the goodliest situation that ever I saw; the city old and decayed; but they are making new walls of stone, which will contain six times their city. Their churches and chapels are the best built, the finest adorned, and the cleanliest kept, of any churches in the world. The people delight much in quintas, which are a sort of country houses, of which there are abundance within a few leagues of the city, and those that belong to the nobility are very fine, both houses and gardens. The nation is generally very civil and obliging. In religion divided, between Papists and Jews. The people generally not handsome. They have many religious houses, and bishopricks of great revenue; and the religious of both sexes are for the most part very strict.

Their fruits of all kinds are extraordinary good and fair; their wine rough for the most part, but very wholesome; their corn dark and gritty; water bad, except some few springs far from the city. Their flesh of all kinds indifferent; their mules and asses extraordinary good and large, but their horses few and naught. They have little wood and less grass.

At my coming away I visited several nunneries, in one whereof I was told, that the last year there was a girl of fourteen years of age burnt for a Jew. She was taken from her mother as soon as she was born, in prison, her mother being condemned, and brought up in the Esperanca; although she never heard, as they did to me affirm, what a Jew was, she did daily scratch and whip the crucifixes, and run pins into them in private; and when discovered confessed it, and said she would never adore that God.

On Thursday, August 25th, 1663,|Footnote: The 25th of August, 1663, fell on a Tuesday.| we set sail for England. On the 4th of September, our style, being Friday, we landed at Deal, all in good health, God be praised!

Saturday 5th, we went to Canterbury, and there tarried Sunday, where we went to church, and very many of the gentlemen of Kent came to welcome us into England.

And here I cannot omit relating the ensuing story, confirmed by Sir Thomas Barton, Sir Arnold Braeme, the Dean of Canterbury, with many more gentlemen and persons of this town.

There lives not far from Canterbury a gentleman, called Colonel Colepeper,|Footnote: Lady Barbara, daughter of Robert Sydney, Earl of Leicester, and widow of Thomas, first Viscount Strangford, married secondly Sir Thomas Colepeper, by whom she had Colonel Colepeper, and a daughter, Roberta Anna, who married Major Thomas Porter, and died issueless, June 16th, 1661, more than two years before Lady Fanshawe was told this story, the circumstances of which she states to have happened only three months previously. The Colonel was a most extraordinary character, and though a man of genius and erudition, was very nearly a madman. A voluminous collection of his MSS. is preserved in the British Museum, whence it appears that he was in the habit of committing his most private thoughts to paper; that there was scarcely a subject to which his attention was not directed; and that the Government and eminent persons were continually tormented with his projects and discoveries, embracing among others the Longitude. His quarrel with the Earl of Devonshire, which led to the imposition upon that nobleman of the exorbitant fine of, L.30,000, is well known. But he was always involved in disputes and law-suits, and not unfrequently he was a prisoner for debt. He filed affidavits in Chancery, denying his sister's marriage, with the view of justifying his refusal to pay her portion to her husband; but the only thing which in any way bears on the anecdote of the vault, is the fact that one of the Colonel's conceits was a plan for embalming dead bodies. The horrible suspicion alluded to by Lady Fanshawe is unsupported by any other statement, and it may be hoped that she was as misinformed on the subject as she was about the time of Mrs. Porter's decease. Part of Colonel Colepeper's papers relate to the particulars of a secret marriage, which he says, in a petition to the Court of Chancery, had taken place between him and the daughter and heiress of Alexander Davies, of Ebury, the widow of Sir Thomas Grosvenor; the unusual engagement into which they entered on the wedding-night; the pretended capture of the lady by the Algerines; his correspondence with the French Government to procure her release; the various attempts to violate her person by one Fordwich; her refusal after her return to England to acknowledge the Colonel as her husband, and his efforts to effect that recognition. His wife's letters to him during his imprisonment, which are preserved in the Harleian MS. 7005, and the account of her efforts to procure his release, exhibit proofs of the most touching and devoted affection, and cannot be read without the highest esteem for her character. She was one of the co-heiresses of the last Lord Frecheville.] whose mother was widow unto the Lord Strangford: this gentleman had a sister, who lived with him, as the world said, in too much love. She married Mr. Porter. This brother and sister being both atheists, and living a life according to their profession, went in a frolic into a vault of their ancestors, where, before they returned, they pulled some of their father's and mother's hairs. Within a very few days after, Mrs. Porter fell sick and died. Her brother kept her body in a coffin set up in his buttery, saying it would not be long before he died, and then they would be both buried together; but from the night after her death, until the time that we were told the story, which was three months, they say that a head, as cold as death, with curled hair like his sister's, did ever lie by him wherever he slept, notwithstanding he removed to several places and countries to avoid it; and several persons told us they had felt this apparition.

On Monday, the 7th of September, we went to Gravesend, and from thence by water to Dorset House, in Salisbury Court, where we stayed fifteen days. The 8th of September, 1663, within two hours after our arrival, we were visited by very many kindred and friends, amongst whom his Grace of Canterbury, who came the next day and dined with us. The same day came the Bishop of Winchester, as did many others of the greatest clergy in England.

Upon the 10th of September, my husband went to Bath, to wait upon his Majesty, who was then there: his Majesty graciously received him, and for a confirmation that he approved his service in his negotiation in Portugal, he was pleased to make him a Privy Counsellor. He was also very graciously received by her Majesty the Queen. Being indisposed with a long journey, my husband fell sick, but it continued but two days, thanks be to God!

On the 17th he went by Cornbury, where the Lord Chancellor then was, and so to London, and, in his absence, I, on the 16th, took a house in Boswell Court, near Temple Bar, for two years, immediately moving all my goods thereto, as well those, which were many, that I had left with my sister Turner in her house in my absence, as those that I brought with me out of Portugal, which were seventeen cart-loads.

Upon Saturday, the 19th, my husband returned from his Majesty, and met me at our new house in Boswell Court.

On Monday, the 21st, being at a great feast at my sister Turner's, where there met us very many of our friends upon the same invitation, whereof Sir John Cutler was one, who after dinner brought me a box, saying, "Madam, this was to go to Portugal, but that I heard your Ladyship was landed." In it there was a piece of cloth of tissue for me, and ribbons and gloves for my children. Whilst we were at dinner, there came an express from Court, with a warrant to swear my husband a Privy Counsellor, from Sir Henry Bennet. The 22nd we went down to Hertfordshire, to my brother Fanshawe's; 24th we dined at Sir John Wats', where we were nobly feasted with great kindness, and to add to my content, I there met with my little girl Betty, whom I had left at nurse within two miles of that place, at my going to Portugal. After being entertained at Sir Francis Boteler's, our very good friend, we went to St. Albans to bed, where, the next day, we bought some coach-horses, and on the 26th we returned to London.

On Tuesday, the 29th, we went again to St. Albans, where my husband bought eight more coach-horses; the same night we returned to London.

On the 1st of October, my husband was sworn a Privy Counsellor, in the presence of his Majesty, his Royal Highness, and the greatest part of his Majesty's honourable Privy Council. On the 3rd, my husband waited on her Majesty the Queen-Mother, who received him with great kindness: the 4th I waited on her Majesty at Whitehall, and there delivered the presents which the Queen-Mother of Portugal had sent her Majesty, who received both them and me in her bed-chamber, with great expressions of kindness. I stayed with her Majesty about an hour and a half, which she spent in asking questions of her mother, brothers, and country; after which I waited on her Majesty in the drawing-room, whereinto the King entered presently after, and I seeing the King, retired to the side of the room, where his Majesty came to me presently, saluting me, and bade me welcome home, with great grace and kindness, asking me many questions of Lisbon and the country.

On Sunday the 4th of October, my husband took his place as Privy Counsellor in the Lords' seat; likewise this day his Grace of Canterbury took his seat, and the Bishop of Winchester, both in the same place: his Grace of Canterbury did his homage to the King. The same day that my husband was sworn a Privy Counsellor, I waited on the Queen-Mother at Somerset House, and the Duke and Duchess of York at St. James's, who all received me with great cheerfulness and grace. On the 7th, the Lord Mayor invited all the Lords of the Privy Council to dinner, among whom was my husband.

The 1st of January 1664, New Year's day, my husband, as Privy Counsellor, presented his Majesty with ten pieces of gold in a purse; and the person that carries it hath a ticket given him of the receipt thereof, from the cupboard of Privy Chamber, where it is delivered to the Master of the Jewel-house, who is thereupon to give him twenty shillings for his pains, out of which he is to give to the servant of the Master of the Jewel-house eighteen-pence.

We received, as the custom is, fifteen ounces of gilt plate for a Privy Counsellor, and fifteen ounces for Secretary of the Latin Tongue; likewise we had the impost of four tuns of wine, two for a Privy Counsellor, and two for a Master of Requests.

January 15th, I took my leave of the King and Queen, who, with great kindness, wished me a good voyage to Spain. Then I waited on the Queen-Mother at Somerset House: her Majesty sent for me into her bed-chamber, and after some discourse I took my leave of her Majesty. Afterwards I waited on their Royal Highnesses, who received me with more than ordinary kindness, and after an hour and a half's discourse with me, saluted me and gave me leave to depart.

On Tuesday, January 19th, my husband carried the Speaker, Sir Edward Turner's eldest son, and my brother Turner, to the King, at Whitehall, who conferred the honour of knighthood on them both, my husband particularly recommending my brother Turner to his Majesty's grace and honour.

On the 20th of January my husband took his leave of his Majesty and all the Royal Family, receiving their dispatches and their commands for Spain, from which hour to our going out of town, day and night, our house was full of kindred and friends taking leave of us; and on Tuesday the 21st, 1664, in the morning, at eight o'clock, did rendezvous at Dorset House, in Salisbury Court, in that half of the house which Sir Thomas Fanshawe then lived in, who entertained us with a very good breakfast and banquet. The company that came thither was very great, as was likewise that which accompanied us out of town. Thus, with many coaches of our family and friends, we took our journey at ten of the clock towards Portsmouth.

The company of our family was my husband, myself, and four daughters; Mr. Bertie, son to the Earl of Lindsey, Lord Great Chamberlain of England; Mr. Newport, second son to the Lord Baron Newport; Sir

Benjamin Wright, Baronet; Sir Andrew King; Sir Edward Turner, Knight, son to the Speaker of the Commons' House of Parliament; and Mr. Francis Godolphin, son to Sir Francis Godolphin, Knight of the Bath. The most part of them went by water.

We lay the first night at Guildford, the second at Petersfield, the third at Portsmouth, where we stayed till the 31st of the same month, being very civilly used there by the Mayor and his brethren, who made my husband a freeman of the town, as their custom is to persons of quality that pass that way; and likewise we received many favours from the Lieutenant-Governor, Sir Philip Honywood, with the rest of the commanders of that garrison. As I said before, we went on board the 31st, being Sunday, the Admiral of the Fleet then setting out, Sir John Lawson, Chief Commander, in his Majesty's ship called the Resolution; there was Captain Berkeley, Commander of the Bristol frigate, Captain Utber, Commander of the Phoenix, Captain Ferne, Commander of the Portsmouth, Captain Moon, Commander of the York, and Sir John Lawson's ketch, commanded by Captain King.

Thus, at ten o'clock, we set sail with a good wind, which carried us as far as Torbay, and then failed us; there we lay till Monday the 15th of February, at nine o'clock at night, at which, it pleasing God to give us a prosperous wind, we set sail, and on the 23rd of February, our style, we cast anchor in Cadiz road, in Spain.

So soon as it was known that we were there, the English Consul with the English merchants all came on board to welcome us to Spain; and presently after came the Lieutenant-Governor from the Governor for the time being, Don Diego de Ibara, to give us joy of our arrival, and to ask leave of my husband to visit him, which Don Diego did within two hours after the Lieutenant's return. The next morning, stilo novo, came in a Levant wind, which blew the fleet so forcibly, that we could not possibly land until Monday, the 7th of March, at 10 o'clock in the morning. Then came the Governor, Don Diego de Ibara, aboard, accompanied by most of the persons of quality of that town, with many boats for the conveyance of our family, and a very rich barge, covered with crimson damask fringed with gold, and Persia carpets under foot. So soon as it was day, we set sail to go nearer the shore. We were first saluted by all the ships in the road, and then by all the King of Spain's forts, which salutation we returned again with our guns.

My husband received the Governor upon deck, and carried him into the round-house, who, as soon as he was there, told my husband, that contrary to the usage of the King of Spain, his Majesty had commanded that his ships and forts should first salute the King of England's Ambassador, and that his Majesty had commanded that both in that place of Cadiz and in all others to the Court of Madrid, my husband and all his retinue should be entertained upon the King's account, in as full and ample manner, both as to persons and conveyance of our goods and persons, as if his Majesty were there in person. My husband and self and children went in the barge, the rest in other barges provided for that purpose.

At our setting off, Sir John Lawson saluted us with very many guns, and as we went near the shore the cannon saluted us in great numbers. When we landed we were carried on shore in a rich chair supported by eight men: we were welcomed by many volleys of shot, and all the persons of quality of that town by the sea-side, among whom was the Governor, did conduct my husband with all his train. There were infinite numbers of people, who with the soldiery did show us all the respect and welcome imaginable. I was received by his Excellency Don Melchor de la Cueva, the Duke of Albuquerque's brother, and the Governor of the garrison, who both led me four or five paces to a rich sedan, which carried me to the coach where the Governor's lady was, who came out immediately to salute me, and whom, after some compliments, I took into the coach with me and my children.

When we came to the house where we were to lodge, we were nobly treated, and the Governor's wife did me the honour to sup with me. That afternoon the Duke of Albuquerque came to visit my husband, and afterwards me, with his brother Don Melchor de la Cueva. As soon as the Duke was seated and covered, he said, 'Madam, I am Don Juan de la Cueva, Duke of Albuquerque, Viceroy of Milan, of his Majesty's privy council, General of the galleys, twice Grandee, the first Gentleman of his Majesty's bed-chamber, and a near kinsman to his Catholic Majesty, whom God long preserve!' and then rising up and making me a low reverence with his hat off, said, 'These, with my family and life, I lay at your Excellency's feet.'

They were accompanied by a very great train of gentlemen. At his going away, he told me his Lady would suddenly visit me. We had a guard constantly waited on us, and sentries at the gate below and at the stairs' head above. We were visited by all the persons of quality in that town. Our house was richly furnished, both my husband's quarter and mine; the worst chamber and bed in my apartment being furnished with damask, in which my chambermaid lay; and throughout all the chambers the floors were covered with Persia carpets. The richness of the gilt and silver plate, which we had in great abundance, as we had likewise of all sorts of very fine household linen, was fit only for the entertainment of so great a Prince as his Majesty, our Master, in the representation of whose person my husband received this great entertainment; yet, I assure you, notwithstanding this temptation, that your father and myself both wished ourselves in a retired country life in England, as more agreeable to both our inclinations.

I must not forget here the ceremony the Governor used to my husband. After supper, the Governor brought the keys of the town to my husband, saying, 'Whilst your Excellency is here, I am no Governor of this town, and therefore desire your Excellency, from me your servant, to receive these keys, and to begin and give the word to the garrison.' This night my husband, with all the demonstrations of his sense of so great an honour, returned his Catholic Majesty, by him, his humble thanks, refusing the keys, and wishing the Governor much prosperity with them, who so well deserved that honour the King had given him. Then the Governor pressed my husband again for the word, which my husband gave, and was this: 'Long live his Catholic Majesty!' Then the Governor took his leave, and his Lady of me, whom I accompanied to the stairs' head.

The next day we were visited by the Mayor and all the Burgesses of the town. On the same day, Saturday the 8th, the Governor's Lady sent me a very noble present of India plate and other commodities thereof. In the afternoon the Duchess of Albuquerque sent a gentleman to me, to know if with conveniency her Excellency might visit me the next day, as the custom of the Court is.

On Sunday the 9th, her Excellency with her daughter, who was newly married to her uncle Don Melchor de la Cueva, visited me. I met them at the stairs' head, and at her Excellency's going, there parted with her. Her Excellency had on, besides other very rich jewels, as I guess, about two thousand pearls, the roundest, the whitest, and the biggest that ever I saw in my life.

On Thursday the 13th, the English Consul with all the merchants brought us a present of two silver basins and ewers, with a hundred weight of chocolate, with crimson taffeta clothes, laced with silver laces, and voiders, which were made in the Indies, as were also the basins and ewers.

This afternoon I went to pay my visit to the Duchess of Albuquerque. When I came to take coach, the soldiers stood to their arms, and the Lieutenant that held the colours displaying them, which is never done to any one but to Kings, or such as represent their persons. I stood still all the while, then at the lowering of the colours to the ground, they received for them a low courtesy from me, and for himself a bow; then taking coach, with very many persons both in coaches and on foot, I went to the Duke's palace, where I was again received by a guard of his Excellency's, with the same ceremony of the King's colours as before. Then I was received by the Duke's brother and near a hundred persons of quality. I laid my hand upon the wrist of his Excellency's right hand; he putting his cloak thereupon, as the Spanish fashion is, went up the stairs, upon the top of which stood the Duchess and her daughters, who received me with great civility, putting me, into every door, and all my children, till we came to sit down in her Excellency's chamber, where she placed me on her right hand, upon cushions, as the fashion of this Court is, being very rich and laid upon Persia carpets.

At my return, the Duchess and her daughter went out before me, and at the door of her Excellency's chamber, I met the Duke, who with his brother and the rest of the gentlemen that did accompany our gentlemen during our stay there, went down together before me. When I took my leave of the Duchess, in the same place where his Excellency received me, the Duke led me down to the coach in the same manner as his brother led me up the stairs; and having received the ceremony of the soldiers, I returned home to my lodgings; where after I had been an hour, Don Antonio de Pimentel, the Governor of Cadiz, who that day was newly come to town, after having been to visit my husband, came to visit me with great company, on the part of his Catholic Majesty, and afterwards upon his own score. He sent me a very rich present of perfumes, skins, gloves, and purses embroidered, with other nacks of the same kind.

Sir John Lawson being now ready to depart from Cadiz, we presented him with a pair of flagons, one hundred pounds, and a tun of Luzena wine, which cost us forty pounds, and a hundred and forty pieces-of-eight for his men. We sent Captain Ferne two hundred pieces-of-eight, and to his men forty pieces-of-eight, they being very careful of our goods, the most of which he brought. We sent Captain Berkeley a hundred pieces-of-eight, and to his men twenty; he carried part of our horses, as did Captain Utber, to whom we sent a like sum.

On the 19th of March, we took our leave of Cadiz, where we gave at our coming away, to persons that attended on us in several offices, two hundred and eighty pieces-of-eight. We were accompanied to the water- side in the same manner. We were received on shore with all points of formality, and having taken our leave, with many thanks and compliments to the Governor, and Don Diego Ibara, his lady, and all the rest of those persons there, to whom we were as much beholden for their civility, we entered the King's barge, which was newly trimmed up for the purpose by the Duke of Medina Celi, at Puerto de Sta Maria. No person ever went in it before but the King. The Governor, Don Antonio de Pimentel, went with us in the barge, and many other barges were provided by him for all our train.

At our going we had many volleys of shot, afterwards many cannons, and as we went, the guns of all the ships in the harbour. When we were come over the bar, all the forts by St. Mary's Port saluted us; and when we came to the shore-side, we found many thousand soldiers in arms, in very great order, with their commanders, and a bridge made on purpose for us, with great curiosity, so far into the river, that the end of the bridge touched the side of the barge. At the end of the bridge stood the Duke of Medina Celi and his son, the Duke of Alcala. During the time of our landing, we had infinite volleys of shot, presented with drums beating and trumpets sounding, and all the demonstration of hearty welcome imaginable.

The two dukes embraced my husband with great kindness, welcoming him to the place, and the Duke of Medina Celi led me to my coach, an honour that he had never done any but once, when he waited on your Queen to help her on the like occasion. The Duke d'Alcala led my eldest daughter, and the younger led my second, and the Governor of Cadiz, Don Antonio de Pimentel, led the third. Mrs. Kestian carried Betty in her arms.

Thus I entered the Duchess of Alcala's coach, which conveyed me to my lodging, the ceremony of the King's colours being performed as at Cadiz. We passed through the streets, in which were an infinite number of people, to a house provided for us, the best of all the place, which was caused to be glazed by the Duke on purpose for us. At our alighting out of the coaches, the Duke led me up into my apartment, with an infinite number of noblemen and gentlemen, his relations; there they took their leave of me, conducting my husband to his quarter, with whom they stayed in visit about half an hour, and so returned to his house. After I had been there three hours, the Duchess of Alcala sent a gentleman to say her Excellency welcomed me to the place, and that, as soon as I was reposed after my long voyage, she would wait upon me: in like manner did the Marquis of Bayona and his lady, and their son with his lady.

I must not pass by the description of the entertainment, which was vastly great, tables being plentifully covered every meal for above three hundred persons. The furniture was all rich tapestry, embroideries of gold and silver upon velvet, cloth of tissue, both gold and silver, with rich Persia carpets on the floors: none could exceed them. Very delicate fine linen of all sorts, both for table and beds, never washed, but new cut out of the piece, and all things thereunto belonging. The plate was vastly great and beautiful, nor for ornament were they fewer than the rest of the bravery, there being very fine cabinets, looking-glasses, tables, and chairs.

On Thursday, at two in the afternoon, the Duchess of Alcala came to visit me; she had lain in but three weeks of a daughter. The day before she performed all the ceremonies and civilities, which is the custom, of the Court to me and mine.

On the 21st I was visited by the Marquesa of Bayona, and all that noble family. On the 23rd I went to repay the Duchess of Alcala her Excellency's visit, and to give her thanks for my noble entertainment; a part thereof being provided under the care of her Excellency.

I likewise went to pay the visit to the Marquesa de Bayona. On Monday the 24th, [Footnote: The new style is here used.] we began our journey from Port St. Mary to Madrid, and taking leave of all the company, we gave one hundred pieces-of-eight to the servants of the family, and fifty pieces-of-eight to the Duke's coachman and footmen. The Duke accompanied me in the same manner as he did when he brought me to the coachside when we landed; and afterwards my husband and the Duke entering the Duke's coach, he brought us a mile out of town, as did also the Marquis of Bayona, and his lady, with an infinite number of persons of the best quality of that place.

That night we went to Xerez, being met, a league before we came to the town, by the Corregidor, accompanied by many gentlemen and coaches of that place, with many thousands of common people, who conducted us to a house provided for us, as the King had commanded, with plenty of all sorts of accommodation. My husband made his entry into the town in the Corregidor's coach, as he did in all places up to Madrid.

At this town I was visited by my Lord Dongan's [Footnote: Sir William Dongan, who was created Baron Dongan and Viscount Dongan of Claine, in the county of Kildare, in the Peerage of Ireland, in 1661. He was raised to the Earldom of Limerick, by James the Second, in 1685, and was attainted in 1691. A letter from him to Sir Richard Fanshawe, dated at Xeres, 1st June 1664, occurs among the Original Letters of Sir Richard Fanshawe, printed in 1701, page 102; and in his correspondence with Lord Arlington, in the British Museum, he thus alluded to him:—MADRID, 3rd June, 1666, stilo loci. "Lord Dongan intends to set forth from this Court to England upon Friday next."- Harl. MS. 7010, f. 274. MADRID, 6th of June, 1665, stilo loci. "The bearer hereof, my Lord Dongan, passing through this Court for England, offered me an opportunity of congratulating your Excellency, &c."— Ibid. f. 276.] lady, who lives there, and whose visit I repaid the next day before I left the town. We received letters by a gentleman, sent express from the Duke of Medina Celi, and the Duke of Alcala, who both wrote to my husband, and his Duchess to me, all of them expressing great civility and kindness. By the bearer of these letters we returned the acknowledgment of their favours in our letters, to all their Excellencies, and presented the knight that brought them with a chain of gold that cost thirty pounds sterling.

At nine o'clock we left the pleasant town of Xerez, and lodged the next night at Lebrija; and the next night at Utrera, where we saw the ruins of a brave town, nothing remaining extraordinary, but the fineness of the situation. We were met there by Don Lope de Mendoca, who was sent with his troop of horse from Seville, by command of the Asistente of that city, [Footnote: The Asistencia of Seville is a high municipal office, peculiar to that city. Dic. de la Acad. Espan.] the Conde de Molina. There came out to meet us also, the Corregidor of Utrera, with an infinite number of persons of all qualities, who met us a league from the town, as did also the English Consul of Seville, with many English merchants, who had clothed twelve footmen in new liveries, to show the more respect to my husband. We were lodged in a priest's house, which was very nobly furnished for our reception, and our treatment was answerable thereunto.

Thursday the 27th of March, we entered Seville, being met a league from the city by the assistant, the Conde de Molina, with many hundred coaches, with nobility and gentry in them, and very many thousands of the burgesses and common people of the town. My husband, after usual compliments passed, went into the Conde's coach. I followed my husband in my own coach, as I ever did in all places; all the pages going next my coach on horseback, and then our coach of state, and other coaches and litters behind, many of the gentlemen and servants riding on horseback, and many of the gentlemen did ride before the coach. Thus we entered that great city that had been, of Seville, though now much decayed. We lay in the King's palace, [Footnote: The Alcazar.] which was very royally furnished on purpose for our reception, and all our treatment during our stay. We were lodged in a silver bedstead, quilt, curtains, valances, and counterpane of crimson damask, embroidered richly with flowers of gold. The tables of precious stones, and the looking-glasses bordered with the same; the chairs the same as the bed, and the floor covered with rich Persia carpets, and a great brasero of silver, filled full of delicate flowers, which was replenished every day as long as we stayed. The hangings were of tapestry full of gold, all which furniture was never lain in but two nights, when his Majesty was at Seville. Within my chamber was a dressing-room, and by that, a chamber very richly furnished, in which my children lay, and within them all my women: on the other side of the chamber as I came in, was my dining-room, in which I did constantly eat. I and my children eating at a table alone, all the way, without any company, till we came to our journey's end, where we provided for ourselves at Ballecas, within a league of Madrid. In this palace, the chief room of my husband's quarters was a gallery, wherein were three pair of Indian cabinets of japan, the biggest and beautifulest that ever I did see in my life: it was furnished with rich tapestry hangings, rich looking-glasses, tables, Persia carpets, and cloth of tissue chairs. This palace hath many princely rooms in it, both above and underneath the ground, with many large gardens, terraces, walks, fish-ponds, and statues, many large courts and fountains, all of which were as well dressed for our reception as art or money could make them.

During our stay in this palace, we were every day entertained with a variety of recreations; as shows upon the river, stage plays, dancing, men playing at legerdemain, which were constantly ushered in with very great banquets, and so finished.

On the 30th, the Malaga merchants of the English presented my husband with a very fine horse, that cost them three hundred pounds. On the 1st of April, the English merchants of Seville, with their Consul, presented us with a quantity of chocolate and as much sugar, with twelve fine sarcenet napkins laced thereunto belonging, with a very large silver pot to make it in, and twelve very fine cups to drink it out of, filigree, with covers of the same, with two very large salvers to set them upon, of silver.

On Thursday the 3rd of April, 1664, we took our leave of the assistant and the rest of that noble company at Seville. The Conde de Molina, who was Asistente of Seville, presented me with a young lion; but I desired his Excellency's pardon that I did not accept of it, saying I was of so cowardly a nature, I durst not keep company with it. In the same manner as they received us, so they accompanied us a league onward on our way, whereupon my husband alighting out of the Conde's coach, and having with me taken leave of all the company, both he and I got upon horseback; and here we took our leave of my Lord Dongan, who with great kindness brought us so far from Xerez. Some of the Malaga merchants of Seville accompanied us on our journey. That night we lay at Carmona; and on the 4th of April at Fuentes, the Onor of the Marquis, who is now at Paris, Ambassador from the King of Spain to that Court. On the 5th we lay at Ezija, where we received noble entertainment from the noblemen and gentlemen of that town; where we stayed till Thursday, the 8th of April, and after paying thanks to those persons that had so well ordered that noble entertainment with great civility to us, we went that night to Cordova, where, a league before we came to the town, we were met by the Corregidor with near a hundred coaches, and a foot company of soldiers stood on each side of the way, giving volleys of shot, with displayed colours and trumpets, with many thousands of people, who by fireworks and other expressions showed much joy. Here we parted with Don Lope, a gentleman sent from the Conde de Molina to this place to accompany us.

We were lodged at a very brave house, and as bravely furnished: at night we had a play acted, and during our stay there we saw many nunneries, and the best churches, as we had likewise done at Seville and at all the other towns through which we had passed in our journey from the seaside. We had there the feast of the bulls, called in the Spanish tongue juego de toros. [Footnote: Properly "corridas de toros" i.e., bull fights.] We had likewise another sport, called juego de canas [Footnote: A kind of tournament played with canes instead of lances.] in which appeared very many fine gentlemen, fine horses, and very fine trappings. We had abundance of entertainments, and yet their civility and good manners exceeded all, as likewise the fame of that place, which is so highly renowned in the world for noble and well-bred gentlemen. The Corregidor presented me with twelve great cases of amber and orange-water, reputed to be the best in the world, with twelve barrels of olives, which have likewise the same fame.

Upon Thursday the 15th of April we took our leave of Cordova, and all those noble persons therein, lodging that night at Carpio, the Marquisship of Don Lewis de Haro; and on the 16th, we lodged at Andujar, and on the 17th at Linares; the 18th we entered the Sierra Morena, and lodged at St. Estevan, the Onor of a Conde, who is at present Vice-King of Peru; on the 19th, we came out of the Sierra Morena, and lodged that night at la Torre de Juan-Abad; on the 20th we lay at La Membrilla, and there stayed all day on Monday and Tuesday; the 22nd at Villarta: here rises the river Guadiana, that goes under ground seven leagues before. On the 23rd, we lay at Consuegra; here Don John of Austria was nursed. The 24th, we lay at Mora; on the 25th, we lay at the famous city of Toledo, two leagues from that town. The Marquis of——, Governor of Toledo, met us, in whose coach my husband went with him towards the town, where within half a league he was met by four persons that represented the city, and all the city of Toledo, with all the noblemen and gentlemen of that town. A little farther the Marquis's lady met me, who alighting out of her coach, and I to meet her, after some compliments passed, I entered her coach with my children, and so passed through the streets, in which there were both water-works and fire-works, and many thousand people of all sorts, and companies of soldiers giving us volleys of shots.

We alighted at the gate, the Marquis leading me up into my lodgings. This house, next to the King's Palace at Seville, was both the largest and the noblest furnished that I saw in all my journey; and likewise all the streets of the city were hung with rich tapestry and other things of silver and gold embroidery, through which we passed. We were there entertained, during our stay, with comedies and music, and juego de toros, and with great plenty of provisions of all sorts, that were necessary to demonstrate a princely entertainment. I eat constantly at a table on purpose provided for me, at which the Marquesa kept me company, as she did likewise whenever I went to visit any remarkable place, of which there are many in Toledo, but none comparable to the great church, which for the greatness and beauty of it I have not seen many better, but for the riches therein never the like. Here my husband received another message from the Duke de Medina las Torres, desiring him to meet him at Valdemoro the Friday following, his Catholic Majesty being then at Aranjuez. This message was sent by a gentleman of his own, the other that he sent to welcome us into this country, being under-gentleman of the horse to her Majesty.

Upon Thursday the 29th of April, we took our leave of the Marquis and his lady, giving one hundred and eighty pieces-of-eight among his family. The night we lay at Yllescas, and on the 30th we came to Ballecas, where we found a house provided for us. Here the King's entertainment ceased, and we provided for all the accommodations of our family, the bare house only excepted. We continued at Ballecas till the 8th of June following, during which time there happened nothing extraordinary; the Duke often sending his secretary to my husband about business, and the Master of the Ceremonies about our constant endeavour to get a house, though at last we were glad to go to a part of a house of the Conde de Irvias, [Footnote: Query] where the Duke of St. Germain had lived before. Here we received many messages of welcome to the Court from all the Ambassadors and all the Grandees, and I from the Ambassadors' ladies, the Duchess de Medina las Torres, with great numbers of the greatest persons of quality in Madrid. The men visited my husband, but I could not suffer the ladies to visit me, though they much desired it, because I was so straitened in my lodgings, which in no sort were convenient to receive persons of that quality in, not being capacious enough for our own family, for whose accommodation we took Count Marcin's house close by this.

On Wednesday the 18th of June, my husband had his audience of his Catholic Majesty; who sent the Marquis de Malpica to conduct him, and brought with him a horse of his Majesty's for my husband to ride on, and thirty more for his gentlemen, and his Majesty's coach with the guard that he was captain of. No Ambassador's coach accompanied my husband but the French, who did it contrary to the King's command; who had before, upon my husband's demanding the custom of Ambassadors accompanying all other Ambassadors that came into this Court at their audience, replied, that although it had been so, it should be so no more; saying, it was a custom brought into this Court within less than these twenty-five years, and that it caused many disputes, for which he would no more suffer it. To this order all the Ambassadors in this Court submitted but the French, whose Secretary told my husband, at his coming that morning, that his Master, the Ambassador, said that his Catholic Majesty had nothing to do to give his Master orders, nor would he obey any of them; and so great was this work of supererogation on the part of the French, that they waited on my husband from the palace home, a compliment till that time never seen before.

About 11 o'clock set forth out of his lodgings my husband thus:—First went all those gentlemen of the town and palace that came to accompany him: then went twenty footmen all in new liveries of the same colour we used to give, which is a dark green cloth with a frost upon green lace; then went my husband's gentlemen, and next before himself his camaradoes two and two:

Mr. Wycherley and Mr. Lorimer,
Mr. Godolphin, Sir Edward Turner,
Sir Andrew King, Sir Benjamin Wright,
Mr. Newport and Mr. Bertie.

Then my husband, in a very rich suit of clothes of a dark fillemorte brocade laced with silver and gold lace, nine laces, every one as broad as my hand, and a little silver and gold lace laid between them, both of very curious workmanship; his suit was trimmed with scarlet taffety ribbon; his stockings of white silk upon long scarlet silk ones; his shoes black, with scarlet shoe-strings and garters; his linen very fine, laced with very rich Flanders lace; a black beaver, buttoned on the left side, with a jewel of twelve hundred pounds value. A rich curious-wrought gold chain, made in the Indies, at which hung the King his Master's picture, richly set with diamonds, cost 300 pounds which his Majesty, in great grace and favour, had been pleased to give him at his coming home from Portugal. On his fingers he wore two rich rings; his gloves trimmed with the same ribbon as his clothes. All his whole family were very richly clothed, according to their several qualities. Upon my husband's left hand rode the Marquis of Malpica, Captain of the German guard, and the Mayor-domo to his Majesty, being that week in waiting: by him went all the German guard, and by them my husband's eight pages, clothed all in velvet, the same colour as our liveries; next them followed his Catholic Majesty's coach, and my husband's coach of state with four black horses, the finest that ever came out of England, none going in this Court [Footnote: i.e., Within the royal residence. Out of the city it was allowed to use six horses, as will be presently seen.] with six but the King himself. The coach was of rich crimson velvet, laced with a broad silver and gold lace, fringed round with a massy silver and gold fringe, and the falls of the boot so rich that they hung almost down to the ground: the very fringe cost almost four hundred pounds. The coach was very richly gilt on the outside, and very richly adorned with brass work, with rich tassels of gold and silver hanging round the top of the curtains round about the coach. The curtains were of rich damask, fringed with silver and gold; the harness for six horses was richly embossed with brass work; the reins and tassels for the horses of crimson silk, silver and gold. This coach is said to be the finest that ever entered Madrid with any Ambassador whatsoever. Next to this followed the French Ambassador's coach; then my husband's second coach, which was of green figured velvet, with green damask curtains, handsomely gilt, adorned on the outside, with harness for six horses, suitable to the same. The four horses were fellows to those that drew the rich coach when we went out of town, using always six. After this followed my husband's third coach, with four mules, being a very good one, according to the fashion of this country. Then followed many coaches of particular persons of this Court.

Thus they rode through the greatest streets of Madrid, as the custom is; and alighting within the palace, my husband was conducted up by the Marquis, all the King's guards attending, through many rooms, in which were infinite numbers of people, as there were in the streets to see him pass to the palace up to a private drawing-room of his Catholic Majesty's, where my husband was received with great grace and favour by his Majesty. My husband, being covered, delivered his message in English, interpreted afterwards by himself in Spanish. After this my husband gave his Catholic Majesty thanks for his noble entertainment from our landing to this Court, to which his Catholic Majesty replied, "That, as well for the great esteem he had ever had for his person, as the greatness of his Master whom he served, he would be always glad to be serviceable to him.'

After my husband's obeisance to the King, and saluting all the grandees there waiting, he was conducted to the Queen; where having stayed in company with her Majesty, the Empress,[Footnote: Philip the Fourth of Spain succeeded his father Philip the Third in 1621, and married his niece, Maria Anna, daughter of his sister of the same name by the Emperor Ferdinand. By her he had issue a son, Charles the Second, who succeeded him in 1665, and died in 1700, and two daughters, Maria Theresa, who married Louis XIV. of France, and Margaret, who was the wife of the Emperor Leopold, and who is consequently spoken of in the Memoirs as the Empress. The ceremony of her marriage by proxy, and her departure for her husband's dominions, are afterwards fully noticed.] and the Prince, took his leave. He returned home in his Majesty's coach, with the Marquis of Malpica sitting at the same end, accompanied by the same persons that went with him, having a banquet ready for them at their return. That day in the evening my husband visited his Excellency the Duke de Medina de las Torres; and the next morning, all the Council of State, as the custom of this Court is.

Upon the 21st, all the Ambassadors at this Court, one after the other, visited my husband, as did also the grandees and nobles; his Excellency the Duke de Medina de las Torres beginning. On the 24th, my husband had a private audience of his Catholic Majesty; on the 27th, I waited on the Queen and the Empress, with my daughters and all my train. I was received at the Buen Retiro by the guard, and afterwards, when I came up-stairs, by the Marquesa of Isincessa,[Footnote: Qu. Inojosa?] the Queen's Camarera Mayor, then in waiting. Through infinite number of people I passed to the Queen's presence, where her Majesty was seated at the upper end under a cloth of state, upon three cushions, and on the left hand the Empress, and three more; the ladies were all standing. After making my last reverence to the Queen, her Majesty and the Empress rising up, and making me a little courtesy, sat down again; then I, by my interpreter, Sir Benjamin Wright, said those compliments that were due from me to her Majesty, to which her Majesty made me a gracious and kind reply. Then I presented my children, whom her Majesty received with great grace and favour; then her Majesty speaking to me to sit, I sat down upon a cushion laid for me, above all the ladies who sat, but below the Camarera Mayor, no woman taking place of her Excellency but princesses. The children sat on the other side, mingled with Court ladies that are maids of honour. Thus having passed half an hour in discourse, I took my leave of her Majesty and the Empress, making reverences to all the ladies in passing. I returned home in the same manner as I came. The next day the Camarera Mayor [Footnote: First Lady of the Queen's Household.] sent to see how I did, in compliment from her Majesty.

On the 9th of July my husband sent Don Pedro Rocca, Master of the Ceremonies, a gold chain, which cost four-score pounds; and, on the 22nd of July, the merchants of Alicant sent us a piece of purple damask, of one hundred and thirty yards, for a present. On Saturday, the 16th of August, we came to the house of Siete Chimeneas, which his Majesty gave us to dwell in, having been the house where the Venetian Ambassador dwelt, and who went out for our accommodation by the King's command.

We settled now our family and tables in order: our own consisted of two courses, of eight dishes each, and the steward's of four. We had our money returned from England by Mr. Goddard, an English merchant living in Madrid, a very honest man and an able merchant. Tuesday the 24th, we dined at the Casa del Campo, a house of his Majesty's, in the garden of which stands a very brave statue of Philip the Second, on horseback. October 4th, we dined at the Prado, another house of his Majesty's, which is very fine, and hath a fine park well stored with deer belonging to it.

October ——, we went privately to see Aranjuez, which was most part of it built by Philip the Second, husband to Queen Mary of England. There are the highest trees, and grow up the evenest, that ever I saw; many of them are bored through with pipes for water to ascend and to fall from the top down one against another; and likewise there are many fountains in the side of this walk, and the longest walks of elms I ever saw in my life. The park is well stored with English oaks and elms, and deer; and the Tagus makes it an island. The gardens are vastly large, with the most fountains, and the best, that ever I saw in my life.

As soon as the Duke heard we were gone thither, he immediately sent orders after us for our entertainment by a post; but we were gone before. Going home by Esquivias, we saw those famous reputed cellars, which are forty-four steps down, where that admirable wine is kept in great tinajas, which are pots holding about five hundred gallons each; and to let you know how strangely they clear their wine, it is by putting some of the earth of the place in it, which way of refining their wine is done no where but here.

October the 14th, the King proclaimed the lowering the vellon money [Footnote: Properly, copper currency, as distinguished from the plata, or silver coinage. Hence the English and French Billon, signifying base money.] to the half; and the pistole, that was this morning at eighty-two reals, was proclaimed to go but for forty-eight, which was above eight hundred pounds loss to my husband.

October the 21st, we went to see the Buen Retiro. The Duke de Medina de las Torres, who has the keeping of this house of the King's from his Majesty, sent two of his gentlemen to show us all that belongs thereunto. The place is adorned with much water and fountains, trees and fine gardens, with many hermitages up and down the place, and a very good house for his Majesty; yet the pictures therein did far exceed the rest, they being many, and all very curious, done by the best hand in the world in their times.

On the 27th of October we went, with all our train, to see the Escurial, the Duke de Medina de las Torres having procured a letter here from the Pope's Nuncio to give me leave to see the convent there, which cannot be seen by any woman without his leave: likewise the Duke did send letters to the Prior, commanding him to assist in showing all the principal parts of that princely fabric, and to lodge us in the lodging of the Duke de Montaldo, the Mayor-domo to her Majesty. We were near eighty persons in company, and five coaches. As soon as we were arrived there, the Prior sent two of his chief friars to welcome us to the Escurial. The friar who met us by command a league before, at a grange house of his Majesty's, and accompanied us to the Escurial, being returned, these friars from the Prior brought us a present of St. Martin's wine and melons, a calf, a kid, two great turkeys, fine bread, apples, pears, cream, with some other fine things of that place. On the 28th, being St. Simon's and Jude's day, we all went early in the morning to see the church, where we were met by the Prior at the door, with all the friars on both sides, who received us with great kindness and respect, and all the choir singing till we came up to the high altar; then all of them accompanied us to the Pantheon, which was, for that purpose, hung full of lights in the branches; there saw I the most glorious place for the covering of the bones of their Kings of Spain that is possible to imagine. I will briefly give you this description.

The descent is about thirty steps, all of polished marble, and arched and lined on all sides with jasper polished; upon the left hand, in the middle of the stairs, is a large vault, in which the bodies of their Kings, and Queens that have been mothers of Kings, lie in silver coffins for one year, until the moisture of their bodies be consumed. Over against this is another vault, in which lie buried the bodies of those Queens that had no sons at their death, and all the children of their Kings that did not inherit. At the bottom of the stairs is the Pantheon, built eighty feet square, and is, I guess, about sixty feet over; the whole lining of it in all places is jasper, very curiously carved, both in figures and flowers and imagery; and a branch for forty lights, which is vastly rich, of silver, and hangs down from the top by a silver chain, within three yards of the bottom, and is made with great art, as is also this curious knot of jasper on the floor, that the reflection of the branch and lights is perfectly there to be seen. The bodies of their Kings lie in jasper stones, supported every coffin by four lions of jasper at the four corners; three coffins and three headstones are set in every arch, which arch is curiously wrought in the roof, and supported by jasper pillars: there are seven arches, and one in the middle at the upper end, and over against the coming in, that contains a very curious altar and crucifix of jasper.

From thence we saw all the convent and the sacristia, in which there were all the principal pieces that ever Titian made, and the hands of many others of the most famous men that then were in the world.

After seeing the convent, and every part thereof, we saw the King's palace, with the apothecary's shop, and all the stillatories, and all belonging thereunto.

The Escurial stands under the side of a very high mountain; it has a very fine river, and a very large park well stored with deer: it is built upon a hill, and you ascend above half a mile through a double row of elm-trees to the house, which is abundantly served with most excellent water and wood for their use. The front has a large platform paved with marble, and railed with a stone baluster round about; the entry of the gate is supported by two marble pillars, each of them of one entire marble, which are near twelve feet high. It is built with seventeen courts and gardens thereunto; every court contains a different office; the whole is built of rough marble, with pillars of the same round the cloisters; and the walls thereof are made so smooth, that the famous Titian hath painted them with stories all over, among others, the story of the battle of Lepanto, and the gallery of the palace also: they have infinite numbers of fountains, both within and without house. It contains a very fine palace, a convent, and a college and hospital, all which are exactly well kept and royally furnished; but I cannot omit saying, that the finest stillatory I ever saw is there, being a very large room shelved round, with glasses sized and sorted upon the shelves, many of crystal gilt, and the rest of Venice glasses, and some of vast sizes; the floor is paved with black and white marble; and in the middle stands a furnace, with five hundred stills around it, with glass like a pyramid, with glass heads. The apothecary's shop is large, very richly adorned with paint, and gilding, and marble; there is an inward room, in which the medicines are made, as finely furnished and beautified as the shop; all the vessels are silver, and so are all the instruments for surgery: nothing is wanted there for that purpose that invention or money can produce.

We were entertained with a banquet at the Prior's lodging; and afterwards returned, accompanied by the friars, to our lodgings, where the Prior made a visit to my husband, and my husband offered to repay it again, sending to him to know if his Reverendissima Senoria would give him leave to wait on him, that night, to thank him for his noble entertainment, although both he and I had done it. The Prior excused the visit, and so we rested that night.

I would not have you that read this book, wonder that I should not more largely describe this so unparalleled fabric in the world; but I do purposely omit the particulars, because they are exactly described in a book written by the friars, and sold in that place, with all the cuts of every particular of the place, and you have it among your father's books. The friars of this convent are of the order of St. Lawrence.

On the 29th, we returned home to our house at Madrid, where on Saturday afternoon my little child, Betty, fell ill of the small-pox, as had done my daughter Ann, in the month of September before; but both of them, God's name be praised! recovered perfectly well, without blemish: but as I could not receive, for want of capacity of room, the ladies of the Court at my lodgings at the Conde de Irvias, so could I not receive them here by reason of the smallpox in the family, and they having twice offered to visit me, and I refused it upon that account.

Thursday 27th November, I went to wait upon the Emperor's Ambassador's lady, at her house; upon the 28th, I went to wait upon the Duchess de Medina de las Torres; and on the 29th, the Emperor's Ambassador's lady came to visit me. The same day the Duchess de Medina de las Torres sent an excuse by Don Alonso, one of the Duke's secretaries, that she could not visit that day, by reason her youngest daughter was fallen sick of a fever. Sunday the 30th of November, I sent to thank the Emperor's Ambassador's lady for the visit the day before, and to see how she did.

Upon the 1st of December, we let our dispense for seventy-two thousand reals vellon, a year, which, at forty-eight reals a pistole, is one hundred and twenty-five pistoles a month: he (the contractor) paid me this sum this day, as he is obliged to do the first day of every month; and likewise to give me for the arrears of the dispense, which was near eleven weeks, fourteen thousand reals.

Upon the 15th of December, was seen here at Madrid a very great blazing star, which to our view appeared with a train of twelve or fourteen yards long: it rose at first in the south-south-east, about twelve o'clock at night, but altered its course during the continuance thereof. Within a fortnight after its expiration, it appeared at six o'clock at night with the rays reversed; it continued in our view till the 23rd day of January.

December the 22nd, which is the Queen of Spain's birth-day, I went to give her Majesty joy thereof, and to the Empress, and to the Prince of Spain, in such form as the custom of this Court is. About this time I had sent me by a Genoese merchant, that was a banker in Madrid, a box of about a yard and a half long, and almost a yard and a half broad, and a quarter and a half deep, covered with green taffety, and bound with a silver lace, with lock and key; within, it was divided into many partitions, garnished with gilt paper, and filled full of the best and choicest sweetmeats, all dry. I never saw any so beautiful and good before or since, besides the curiosity.

On the 23rd, we were invited to see a show, performed by forty-eight of the chiefest of the nobility of this Court, who ran two and two on horseback, as fast as the horses could run, in walks railed in on purpose on both sides, before the palace-gate; over which, in a balcony, sat the King, the Queen, and Empress; round about, in other balconies, sat the nobility of the Court, and in an entre-suelo, at the King's left hand, sat the chief of the Ambassadors. My husband and I were with the Duke and Duchess de Medina de las Torres, in their own particular quarter in the palace, which we chose as the best place, and having the best view, whereupon we refused the balcony. The sight was very fine, and the noblemen and horses very richly attired.

Upon the 1st of January, I received of our Dispensero, as was my due, six thousand reals, for the month's dispense, and six thousand more in part of arrears. Upon the 4th of January I waited on the Queen, Prince, and Empress, to give them the buenas pascuas [Footnote: Compliments of the season.] as the custom of this Court is.

On the 5th, here came, among other diversions of sports we had this Christmas, Juan Arana, the famous comedian, who here acted about two hours to the admiration of all that beheld him, considering that he was near upon eighty years of age. About this time the Duke of Alva sent my husband a fat buck; I never eat any better in England. We do take it for granted in England that there is nothing good to eat in Spain, but I assure you the want is money alone.

The 11th of December, the President of Castile gave a warrant to an officer to execute upon Don Francisco de Ayala, to carry him prisoner for some offences by him committed. This gentleman lived in a house within the protection of my husband's barriers, very near to his own dwelling-house; for which reason, no person can give or execute a warrant for what crime soever, without the leave of the Ambassador; but notwithstanding, the officer who executed this warrant, being backed by the President of Castile, did seize the person of Don Francisco de Ayala in his own house, and carried him to prison.

Notice whereof being given to my husband from him, my husband immediately wrote a letter to the President of Castile, demanding the prisoner to be immediately brought home to his house; that he would not suffer the privilege of the King, his master, to be broken, making further greater complaint of this usage to him; to which the next day, in a letter, the President replied, that an Ambassador had no power to protect out of his own house and household, with many other ridiculous excuses; but all his allegations being proved against him, both by ancient and modern custom, by hundred of examples, and nothing left him to defend himself but his own peevish wilfulness, my husband pursued the business with much vigour, telling the gentleman that brought him the President's letter, that his master, the President, as to him had once been very civil, but as to the King, his master, most uncivil, both in the acting and defending so indecent a business; for which reason he would not give an answer by letter to the President, because his to the Ambassador did not deserve one; all which my husband desired the gentleman to acquaint the President, his master, with. Then my husband visited the gentleman in prison, a thing never before known of an Ambassador; telling the prisoner openly, before many gentlemen that were there accompanying of him, that he would have him out, or else that he would immediately leave the Court. The great number of gentlemen and servants of my husband's family gave apprehensions to the keeper of the prison, when my husband demanded leave to visit the prisoner.

The next day, being the 16th, Don Francisco de Ayala was visited, by my husband's example, by most of the council and nobility of this Court. In the evening, in a letter to the Duke de Medina de las Torres, my husband inclosed a memorial to his Catholic Majesty, demanding the prisoner, saying, he was very sorry that at one time, a few years ago, in the year 1650, some English gentlemen, whereof Mr. Sparks was one, did kill one Askew, an agent of Oliver's to the Catholic King. When they had thus done, all those persons and degrees made their escape but Mr. Sparks, who took sanctuary in one of their churches; notwithstanding which, the privilege thereof being defended both by the Archbishop of Toledo and the greatest prelates of this kingdom, he was by the King and council pulled out of the church and executed, so great at that time was the fear that this Court had of Oliver; and now, violation of privileges should only have been used to his Majesty, the King of England, assuring his Majesty he neither could nor would put it up without ample restitution made.

Upon the perusal of this memorial, his Catholic Majesty did immediately command the President of Castile to send his warrant the next day, and to release Don Francisco de Ayala, and to send him home immediately to my husband, which was done accordingly that night; and my husband, with all his coaches and family, which were near a hundred persons, carried him and placed him in his own house before the officers' faces that brought him home from prison. All this you will find in your father's transactions in his Spanish embassy. In this action my husband did not receive so much content in the victory as the Spaniards of all sorts, on whom it made a very great impression; though the chief Minister of state in our country did not value this, nor give the encouragement to such a noble action as was due. And here I will impartially say, what I have observed of the Spanish nation, both in their principles, customs, and country.

I find it a received opinion that Spain affords not food either good or plentiful: true it is that strangers that neither have skill to choose, nor money to buy, will find themselves at a loss; but there is not in the Christian world better wines than their midland wines are especially, besides sherry and canary. Their water tastes like milk; their corn white to a miracle, and their wheat makes the sweetest and best bread in the world; bacon beyond belief good; the Segovia veal much larger and fatter than ours; mutton most excellent; capons much better than ours. They have a small bird that lives and fattens on grapes and corn, so fat that it exceeds the quantity of flesh. They have the best partridges I ever eat, and the best sausages; and salmon, pikes, and sea-breams, which they send up in pickle, called escabeche [Footnote: "Escabeche; a pickle made of white wine, bay leaves, sliced lemons, and spices, used for preserving fish and other food."—Dic. de la Acad. Esp.] to Madrid, and dolphins, which are excellent meat, besides carps, and many other sorts of fish. The cream, called nata, is much sweeter and thicker than any I ever saw in England; their eggs much exceed ours; and so all sorts of salads, and roots, and fruits. What I most admired are, melons, peaches, burgamot pears, grapes, oranges, lemons, citrons, figs, and pomegranates; besides that I have eaten many sorts of biscuits, cakes, cheese, and excellent sweetmeats I have not here mentioned, especially manger-blanc; and they have olives, which are no where so good; and their perfumes of amber excel all the world in their kind, both for household stuff and fumes; and there is no such water made as in Seville.

They have daily curiosities brought from Italy and the Indies to this Court, which, though I got my death-wound in, without partiality, I must say, is the best established, but our own, in the Christian world that I ever saw; and I have had the honour to live in seven. All Ambassadors live in as great splendour as the most ambitious can desire, and if they are just and good, with as much love as they can deserve.

In the Palace none serve the King and Queen but the chiefest of the nobility and ancientest families; no, not in the meanest offices.

The nation is most superstitiously devout in the Roman Catholic religion; true in trust committed to them to a miracle, withstanding all temptations to the contrary, and it hath been tried, particularly about Cadiz and St. Lucar, that for eight or ten pieces-of-eight, poor men will undertake stealing for the merchants their silver aboard when their shipping come in, which sometimes by the watch for that purpose are taken; and after their examination and refusal to declare whose the silver is, or who employed them to steal, they are oftentimes racked, which they will suffer with all the patience imaginable; and notwithstanding their officers, as they execute their punishment, mingle great promises of reward if they will confess, yet it was never known that any ever confessed; and yet these men are not worth ten pounds in the world.

They are civil to all as their qualities require, with the highest respect, so that I have seen a grandee and a duke stop their horse when an ordinary woman passeth over a kennel, because he would not spoil her clothes; and put off his hat to the meanest woman that makes a reverence, though it be their footman's wife. They meddle with no neighbour's fortune or person, but their own families; and they are punctual in visits, men to men, and women to women. They visit not together, except their greatest ministers of state, so public ministers' wives from princes. If they have animosities concerning place, they will by discretion avoid ever meeting in a third place, and yet converse in each other's houses, all the days of their lives, with satisfaction on both sides. They are generally pleasant and facetious company; but in this their women exceed, who seldom laugh, and never loud; but the most witty in repartees, and stories, and notions in the world. They sing, but not well, their way being between Italian and Spanish; they play on all kinds of instruments likewise, and dance with castanuelas very well. They work but little, but very well, especially in monasteries. They all paint white and red, from the Queen to the cobbler's wife, old and young, widows excepted, who never go out of close mourning, nor wear gloves, nor show their hair after their husband's death, and seldom marry. They are the finest-shaped women in the world, not tall, their hair and teeth are most delicate; they seldom have many children; there are none love cleanliness in diet, clothes, and houses more than they do. They dress up their oratories very fine with their own work and flowers.

They have a seed which they sow in the latter end of March, like our sweet basil; but it grows up in their pots, which are often of China, large, for their windows, so delicately, that it is all the summer as round as a ball and as large as the circumference of the pot, of a most pleasant green, and very good scent.

They delight much in the feasts of bulls and stage plays, and take great pleasure to see their little children act before them in their own houses, which they will do to perfection; but the children of the greatest are kept at great distance from conversing with their relations and friends, never eating with their parents but at their birth. [Footnote: i.e., on their birthdays.] They are carried into an apartment with a priest, who says daily the office of their church; a governess, nurse, and under-servants, who have their allowance according to the custom of great men's houses, so many pounds of flesh, fruit, bread, and the like, with such a quantity of drink, and so much a year in money. Until their daughters marry, they never stir so much as down stairs, nor marry for any consideration under their own quality, which to prevent, if their fortunes will not procure husbands, they make them nuns. They are very magnificent in houses, furniture, pictures of the best, jewels, plate, and clothes; most noble in presents, entertainments, and in their equipage; and when they visit, it is with great state and attendance. When they travel, they are the most jolly persons in the world, dealing their provisions of all sorts to every person they meet when they are eating.

One thing I had like to have forgotten to tell you. In the palace there never lies but one person in the King's apartment, who is a nobleman, to wait the King's commands; the rest are lodged in apartments at further distance, which makes the King's side most pleasant, because it is most airy and sweet. The King and Queen eat together twice a week in public with their children, the rest privately, and asunder. They eat often, with flesh to their breakfast, which is generally, to persons of quality, a partridge and bacon, or capon, or some such thing, ever roasted, much chocolate, and sweetmeats, and new-laid eggs, drinking water either cold with snow, or lemonade, or some such thing. Their women seldom drink wine, their maids never; they all love the feasts of bulls, and strive to appear gloriously fine when they see them.

Upon February the 11th, the Emperor's Ambassador's lady visited me. Upon Thursday the 19th of February, went from us to England, Mr. Charles Bertie, Mr. Francis Newport, Sir Andrew King, Sir Edmund Turner, Mr. Francis Godolphin, Mr. Wycherley, Mr. Hatton, and Mr. Smith, with all their servants. This day likewise we received letters of the arrival of Mr. Price from Elvas, a gentleman of my husband's, who had been sent by him on the 28th of January last past to the King of Portugal, upon business of state.

Upon the 2nd of March, we went to see a country house of the Marquesa de Liche, who presented me with a dog and bitch, perfect greyhounds, and I could put each of them in my pocket.

On Thursday the 5th, I returned the visit of the Emperor's Ambassador's lady. March the 8th, we went to see a house of Don Juan de Congro, at Chamartin.

On Wednesday the 19th, we went to take the air, and dined at Vicalvaro. Mr. Price came from Lisbon this day to Madrid.

Upon the 20th of March 1665, stilo novo, upon desire of the Duchess de Medina de las Torres, who was then sick, and had long kept her bed, I visited her Excellency, taking all my children with me. After I had been there a little while, passing those compliments, her Excellency told me that her Catholic Majesty had commanded her to assure me that her Majesty had a very high esteem for me, not only as I was the wife of a great King's Ambassador, for whom her Majesty had much respect, but for my person, and the delight her Majesty took in my conversation, assuring me from her Majesty that, upon all occasions, I should find her most cheerfully willing to do me all possible kindness in her Court; and for a token thereof, her Majesty had herewith sent me a jewel of diamonds, that cost the Queen eight thousand five hundred and fifty ducats, plate, [Footnote: See note, p. 179.] which is about two thousand pounds sterling; which then her Excellency did deliver to me, saying she thought herself much honoured, and much contented, that her Majesty had employed her in a business in which she took so much delight.

I desired her Excellency to lay me at the feet of her Majesty, and to tell her Majesty that I esteemed the honour according as I ought, of whose bounty and graces I and mine had abundantly received ever since our coming into this kingdom. That the ribbon, wherewith the jewel was tied, coming from her Majesty, was a favour of which I should have bragged all the days of my life, though I could never have deserved it; much more did I esteem so rich a jewel her Majesty was pleased to send me; but, above all, her Majesty's gracious acceptance of my service, and her Majesty's promise of her grace and favour to me, in which I desired I might live, giving her Excellency many thanks for the kindness on her part therein, believing that her Excellency had, upon all occasions, made my best actions seem double, and winked at my imperfections, but that which I did certainly know, and desired her Excellency to believe, was, that I was her Excellency's most humble servant.

On Tuesday the 24th of March, the Marquesa de Liche visited me, who had not made a visit before in seven years. On Thursday the 26th, I returned the visit to her Excellency the Marquesa, who entertained me with a very fine banquet, and gave to my youngest girl, Betty, a little basket of silver plate, very richly wrought.

On Thursday the 8th of April, being his Catholic Majesty's birthday, I went to give the Empress and her Catholic Majesty the parabien [Footnote: Congratulation.] thereof, and likewise my thanks to her Majesty for the many honours she had done me, and particularly for that of the jewel.

Upon the 5th of April here appeared a new blazing star, rising in the east about two o'clock in the morning, rising every day a quarter of an hour later than the former, so that it appeared to our view but about three weeks, because the daylight obscured.

Thursday the 23rd of April, we dined at a pleasure-house of the King's, three leagues from Madrid, called the Torre del Prado. Monday, 26th of April, we went to see a garden-house of the Marquis de Liche, which had been the Marquis of Fuentes'. The house was finely adorned with curious pictures painted on the wall, with a very fine and large garden thereunto belonging, in which on many days following we dined.

On Saturday the 3rd of May we heard, by letters from my father, the sad news of the death of my good brother-in-law, my Lord Fanshawe; and, at the same time, of his son's being happily married to one of the daughters and heirs of Sir John Evelyn, of Wiltshire, and widow of Sir John Wray, of Lincolnshire.

May the 28/18th, we went to see the feast of bulls, in a balcony made at the end of a street that looked in even with the row of houses. On the King's right hand, just below the Councils, which is over against all other Ambassadors, there sat the Pope's Nuncio, and the rest of the Ambassadors below him; but we not owning the Pope's priority, your father was placed by himself.

June the 20th, came to this Court by an express, the news of the total rout of the King of Spain's army, commanded by the Marquis of

Caracena, by the Portuguese.[Footnote: At Montesclaros, where the Portuguese were commanded by the Marquis de Marialva.]

Upon the 6th of July, went to the feast of bulls again.

Upon the 7th, anno 1665, came to my husband the happy news of our victory against the Dutch, fought upon the 13th of June, stilo novo.

August the 6th, at eleven o'clock in the morning, was born my son, Richard Fanshawe, God be praised! and christened at four of the o'clock that afternoon by our Chaplain, Mr. Bagshaw: his godfathers my cousin Fanshawe, Chief Secretary, and Mr. Cooper, Gentleman of the Horse: his godmother, Mrs. Kestian, one of my gentlewomen. The same day the Duke of Medina and his Duchess sent to give us joy. Upon the 7th the Duke came in person to give us joy, with all his best jewels on, as the custom of Spain is, to show respect.

Upon Thursday the 10th of August, the Queen sent her Majesty's Mayor-domo, the Marquis of Aytona, to visit me from her Majesty, and to give me joy. The next day her Majesty's Camarera Mayor and the Princess Alva gave me joy, as did likewise most of the others of the greatest ladies at court.

'Oh, ever living God, through Jesus Christ, receive the humble thanks of thy servant for thy great mercy to us in our son, whom I humbly desire thee, O Jesus, to protect; and to make him an instrument of thy glory. Give him thy Holy Spirit, O God, to be with him all the days of his life; direct him through the narrow paths of righteousness, in faith, patience, charity, temperance, chastity, and a love and liking of thy blessed will, in all the various accidents of this life: this with what outward blessings thou, O Heavenly Father, knowest needful for him, I beg of thee, not remembering his sins nor the sins of us his parents, nor of our forefathers, but thy tender mercy, which thou hast promised shall be all over thy works, and for the blessed merits of our only Lord and Saviour Jesus Christ; to whom with thee and the blessed Spirit be all honour and glory, as it was in the beginning, is now, and ever shall be. Amen.'

On Thursday the 17th of September, died Philip the Fourth of Spain having been sick but four days, of a flux and fever. The day before his death he made his will, and left the government of the King and kingdom in the hands of his Queen, Donna Ana of Austria; and to assist her Majesty, he recommended for her council therein, the President of Castile, Conde de Castilla, the Cardinal of Toledo, the Inquisitor General, the Marquis of Aytona, the Vice-Chancellor of Aragon, and the Conde de Penaranda. He declared for his successor, Charles Second, who now reigns; and in case that he should die without issue, the Emperor, if he marries the Infanta, now called the Empress, to whom he is affianced; but if not, the Infanta before himself; after the Emperor, the Duke of Savoy; the Queen of France to inherit next to the Infanta, in case she be a widow, and all her children successively by any other husband; but neither she can inherit nor any child of France.

The body of Philip the Fourth lay exposed from the 18th of September till Saturday night the 19th, in a great room in his palace at Madrid, where he died; in which room they used to act plays. The room was hung with fourteen pieces of the King's best hangings, and over them rich pictures round about, all of one size, placed close together. At the upper end of the room was raised a throne of three steps, upon which there was placed a bedstead, boarded at the bottom, and raised at the head: the throne was covered with a rich Persia carpet; the bottom of the bedstead was of silver, the valance and head-cloth, for there were no curtains, were cloth of gold, wrought in flowers with crimson silk. Over the bedstead was placed a cloth of state, of the same with the valance and head-cloth of the bedstead; upon which stood a silver-gilt coffin, raised about a foot or more higher at the head than at the feet, in which was laid a pillow, and in the coffin lay Philip the Fourth, with his head on the pillow, upon it a white beaver hat, his head combed, his beard trimmed, his face and hands painted. He was clothed in a musk colour silk suit, embroidered with gold, a golilla (or ruff) about his neck, cuffs on his hands, which were clasped on his breast, holding a globe and a cross on it therein; his cloak was of the same, with his sword by his side; stockings, garters, and shoe-strings of the same, and a pair of white shoes on his feet. In the room were erected six altars for the time, upon which stood six candlesticks, with six wax candles lighted, and in the middle of each altar a crucifix; the forepart of each altar was covered with black velvet, embroidered with silver. Before the throne a rail went across from one side of the room to the other. At the two lower corners of the throne, at each side, stood a nobleman, the one holding an imperial crown, the other the sceptre; and on each side of the throne six high candlesticks with six tapers in them. The doors of that room were kept by the Mayor-domo of the King and Queen then in waiting, and the outward by the Italian guard.

On the Saturday night, he was carried upon a bier, hung betwixt two mules, upon which the coffin with the King's body was laid, covered with a covering of cloth of gold, and at every corner of the bier was placed a high crystal lanthorn with lighted tapers in it. He was attended by some grandees, who rode next after him, and other noblemen in coaches, with between two and three hundred on horseback, of whom a great part carried tapers lighted in their hands: this was the company, besides footmen. When the King's body came to the Convent of the Escurial, the friars of that convent stood at the gate, and there, according to the institution of the place, performed the ceremonies as follow. The priors asked the grandees, who carried the King on their shoulders, for none other must touch him, 'Who is in that coffin, and what do they there demand?' Upon which the Sumiller de Corps, [Footnote: Properly, the Groom of the Stole; "a cuyo cargo esta la asistencia al Rey en su retrete."—Dic. de la Acad.] who is the Duke de Medina de las Torres, answered, 'It is the body of Philip the Fourth of Spain, whom we here bring for you to lay in his own tomb.' Upon which the Duke delivered the Queen's letter, as Regent of the kingdom, to testify that it was her Majesty's command that the King's body should be there buried. Then the Prior read the letter, and accompanied the body before the high altar, where it was for some time placed, till they had performed the usual ceremonies for that time appropriated. After which the grandees took up the corpse again, and carried it down into the Pantheon, into which as soon as they were entered, the Prior demanded of the Duke the covering of the King's body as his fee.

Then demanded he the keys, upon which the Duke delivered him his, as Sumiller de Corps, and then the Prior's own sent him by the Queen, and the Mayor-domo then in waiting delivered him his. The Prior having received these three keys, demanded franca [Footnote: i.e., puerta franca; admittance.] of the Duke and Mayor-domo, that in that coffin was the body of Philip the Fourth; and when they had done, they there left the body with the Prior, who after the body's lying some time in the place where the infants are buried, placed it in his own tomb.

My husband with all his family and coaches were put into mourning for Philip the Fourth of Spain.

October the 4th following, I waited upon the Queen to give her Majesty pesame [Footnote: Compliments of condolence.] of the King's death, who received me with great grace and favour, as likewise did the King and the Empress, who were both present.

On the 8th of October my husband and I, with all our family and son, being the first time he went out of doors, went to the Plaça Mayor, to hear and see King Charles the Second proclaimed by the Duke de Medina de las Torres, who was very richly apparelled in a silk suit, embroidered with silver and gold, set with diamond buttons: he was accompanied by most of the nobles in the town on horseback, as he himself was. In his right hand he carried the King's royal standard, and by his left side rode the Mayor of the town. The Heralds that rode before went first upon the scaffold, which was there made for that purpose before the King's balcony, where he was wont to see the juego de toros. The scaffold was covered with carpets. On each side of the Duke stood the Heralds, and on his left hand stood the Mayor, and by the Heralds two Notaries. The King was proclaimed in five places; at the Court above named, at the Descalcas Reale, at the Town House, at the Gate of Guadajara, and at the Palace.

November the 9th, I went to give the Queen the parabien of the King's birth-day, who, the 6th of this month, completed four years of age. Her Majesty received me with great grace and favour, causing the King to come in and receive of me the parabien of his anos likewise.

The 14th of this month I went to wait on the Camerara Mayor and the Marquis de los Velez, the King's Aya, [Footnote: Governor or tutor.] from both of whom I received great kindnesses.

December the 17th, 1665, my husband, upon the part of our King his master, and the Duke de Medina de las Torres, on the part of his Catholic Majesty, did conclude and signed together the peace between England and Spain, and the articles for the adjustment between Spain and Portugal, which articles were cavilled at by the Lord Chancellor Clarendon and his party, that they might have an opportunity to send the Earl of Sandwich out of the way from the Parliament, which then sat, and who, as he and his friends feared, would be severely punished for his cowardice in the Dutch fight. He neither understood the customs of the Court, nor the language, nor indeed any thing but a vicious life; and thus was he shuffled into your father's employment to reap the benefit of his five years' negotiation of the peace between England, Spain, and Portugal: and after above thirty years studying state affairs, and many of them in the Spanish Court: so much are Ambassadors slaves to the public ministers at home, who often, through envy or ignorance, ruin them!

December the 23rd, I went to give the Queen the parabien of her anos, whereof she had completed thirty-one. I likewise gave joy to the Empress and the King, who were both then present.

The 6th of January, 1666, twelfth-day, stilo novo, my husband sent Mr. John Price, one of his secretaries, to Lisbon, to advertise that King, by the Conde de Castel Melhor, of his intended journey the week following. On the 14th of this present January, the Duke of Medina de las Torres wrote a letter to my husband, by the command of her Catholic Majesty, which said, that for the great kindness and pains he had and did take for the accommodating a peace between England and Spain, and procuring a truce for thirty years between the crowns of Spain and Portugal, that, on the day of the ratification thereof, her Majesty did give him [Footnote: These gratifications were never paid, because my Lord Sandwich was sent to receive what advantage he could make. But the body of the peace being concluded before by my husband, he received very small advantage thereby; but had my husband lived, he would, through their justice and kindness to him, for his great wisdom and indefatigable pains in procuring a triple peace between the three crowns of England, Spain, and Portugal, have received a sum.] an hundred thousand pieces-of-eight, and likewise for a further expression of her Majesty's kindness, to me fifty thousand pieces-of- eight.

The 16th of January, 1666, being twelfth-day, English account, my husband began his journey from Madrid to Portugal. The day before he went, her Catholic Majesty sent the Marquis Aytona to offer a set of her Majesty's machos to carry his litter, and another set for his coach, but my husband refused both, with many humble thanks to her Majesty for so great grace and honour done him, which he refused upon no other score but the consideration of the length of the journey, and the badness of the way, which the time of the year caused, which would expose the beasts to that hazard, as he could not satisfy himself to put them in; and although my husband was next day pressed again to receive this favour, yet he refused it with much respect to her Majesty, for the forenamed reasons. Likewise the Duke de Medina de las Torres sent two sets of very brave machos to convey my husband to Portugal, which he refused with many thanks to his Excellency, upon the same account he had done those formerly to her Majesty. My husband carried none of his own horses or mules, but hired all he used for himself or his retinue. He went in his own litter, and carried one of his own coaches with him, and five sumpters, covered with his own sumpter cloths. His retinue were:—Mr. Fanshawe, Chief Secretary; Mr. Price, gone before to Lisbon; Mr. Cooper, Gentleman of the Horse; Mr. Bagshawe, Chaplain; Mr. Ashburnham, Mr. Parry, Mr. Creighton, Mr. Eyres, Steward; Mr. Weeden, Mr. Jemmet, Mr. Bumstead, Pages; Mr. Hellow, Butler; William, a Cook; Francis, a Groom; Frances, a Laundress, and four Spanish footmen. To every five mules went a moco, and a sobrestante over all. Her Majesty sent an alguazil of the court with my husband through Spain, to provide him lodgings, and to assist him in all other occasions belonging to his journey. I accompanied my husband a league out of town in our coach of state; then he entered his litter, and so began his journey.

Within an hour after I was returned to my house, the Duke and Duchess de Medina de las Torres sent each of them a gentleman with very kind messages to me on the part of their Excellencies.

The 17th, came the Master of the Ceremonies to see me, and offered the services of this Court, with high compliments and much kindness; the 18th, came the Duke of Aveyro to see me, and afterwards the Marquis of Trucifal; the 19th, came to see me the Baron of L'Isola's lady; the 20th of January, I received a letter from my husband at Toledo; the 26th, the Marquis de Liche came to visit me; the 28th, the Duchess de Aveyro sent a gentleman to me, to excuse her not coming to see me, by reason of her being with child, and not having stirred out of her chamber from the time she had conceived with child; the 29th I received a letter from my husband, from Frexenal.

The 2nd of February, the Duke de Medina de las Torres sent to me Don Nicolas Navas, with letters from her Catholic Majesty herself to my husband, and putting up the packet here before me, inclosed my letters therein, I giving a cover, and sealing it with my seal, and a passport to the post that carried it, to come and go: all which was required of me by his Excellency, who was pleased to continue this for me every post that he sent during my husband's stay in Portugal.

The 12th of February, the Duchess of Albuquerque sent a gentleman to excuse her not visiting me, her Excellency being sick of a fever. This night likewise the Duke sent a second post to my husband as before. The 13th, Father Patricio came to visit me, from the Duke; the 17th died the Queen-mother of Portugal; the 20th, the Duke despatched a third post to my husband. The 23rd, the Duke and his Duchess came to visit me in very great state, having six coaches and two sedans to wait on them, and above a hundred gentlemen and attendants. The 27th, one of the three posts returned from my husband; another on the 2nd of March; the third on the 10th.

On the 8th of March, 1666, stilo novo, my husband returned from Lisbon to this Court, with all his family in very good health, God be praised! I went with my children two leagues out of town, to Ricon, to meet him. He brought in his company Sir Robert Southwell, an enviado from our King to Portugal and Spain, if need so required. My husband entertained him at his house three weeks and odd days.

Upon the 26th of March, came a letter from Coruna, advertising this Court of the Earl of Sandwich's arrival, as Extraordinary Ambassador from our King to his Catholic Majesty.

Sunday the 12th of April, I took my leave of the Queen of Spain, and Empress, and the King, and the next day of the Camarera Mayor, and of the King's Aya.

The 13th of April, returned from hence a gentleman named Mr. Weeden, who came hither on the 6th of the same month, bringing letters to this Court and my husband from his Lord, the Earl of Sandwich, and likewise a list of the Extraordinary Ambassador's family, which was as follows:—

Mr. Sidney Montague, his son; Sir Charles Herbert, Mr. Steward, Mr. Godolphin, Secretary to the Embassy; Mr. Worden, Mr. Bedles, Mr. Cotterrel, Mr. Bridges, Mr. Clarke, Mr. Melham, Mr. Stuard, Mr. Linch, Mr. Boddie, Interpreter; Mr. Parker, Mr. Shere, Mr. Moore, Chaplain; The Steward; Captain Ferrer, Gentleman of the Horse; Mr. William Ferrer, Mr. Gateley, Clergyman; Mr. Gibbs, Mr. Boreman, Clerk of the Kitchen; Mr. Lond, Mr. Veleam, Mr. Mallard; Mr. Richard Jarald, Mr. Joseph Chaumond, Under Secretaries; Francis Paston, Confectioner; Henry Pyman, Butler; Gentleman, Mr. Cooke; Balfoure and Attenchip, two Cooks; Allion Thompson, Trumpeter; William Killegrew, Thomas Rice, William Rich, Francis Warrington, James Ashton, Mr. Place, John Beverley, Briggs, Richard Cooper, Mr. Kerke, Mr. Churchill, Mr. Jeffereys, Mr. Crown, Pages, ten; Mr. Nicholas Neto, Mr. Righton, Edward Hooton, Richard Russel, Andrew Daniel; Peacock, Dennis, Footmen; Thomas Gibson, Thomas Williams, Josias Brown, Caspar, el negro; Nathaniel Bennet; the Nurse, her Husband, two Maids, Nicholas Bennet, Henry Mitchell, and John Goods.

On the 14th I took my leave of the Duchess de Medina de las Torres, the Marquesa de Trucifal, and the Condessa de Torres Vedras. On the 15th, I took my leave of the Duchess de Aveiro, who gave my daughter Katharine a jewel of twenty-seven emeralds; and to my daughter Margaret a crystal box set in gold, and a large silver box of amber pastilles to burn; and to my daughter Ann a crystal bottle, with a gold neck, full of amber water, and a silver box of filagree; and to my daughter Betty a little trunk of silver wire, made in the Indies. This day I likewise visited the Marquesa de Liche, and daughter-in-law of the Almirante of Castilla, the Baron de L'Isola's lady, and Don Diego Tinoco's lady, who had all visited me.

On the 16th, I took my leave of the Duchess of Albuquerque, and her Excellency Donna Maria de la Cueva. The Duchess showed me a large room full of gilt and silver plate, which they said cost a hundred thousand pistoles, though to my eye it did not seem of half the worth. It was made for the Duke's journey into Germany, being the principal person entrusted to dispose of her Imperial Majesty's family and money for a voyage to that Court; and afterwards he and his lady are to return to Sicily, and there to remain Viceroy. The same day I took my leave of the German Ambassador's lady. Easterday being the 25th of April, 1666, the Infanta Donna Maria was married to the Emperor by proxy, viz., the Duke de Medina de las Torres.

THE CEREMONY

First went a great high coach of the Duke's, drawn by four black Flanders' mares; in it were the Duchess's two sons, with other persons of quality. In Madrid none can go with six horses but the King or Queen, as I said before. Then went the Duke's coach, a most exceeding rich one, drawn by four grey Flanders' mares, in the upper end whereof the Duke himself sat, with the German Ambassador on his right hand, the Duke of Alva on his left, in the other end the Conde de Penaranda, between the Duke of Pastrana and his son. After this coach followed immediately the Duke of Medina's Gentleman of the Horse, upon a very fine white one. Then went a very rich new coach, empty, of the German Ambassador's, made on purpose for the day, drawn by four horses. Then followed another of the Duke's coaches with some of his gentlemen in it; then the German Ambassador's second coach, with some of his gentlemen in it. Then one of the Duke's coaches, in which was the Baron de Lesley, Envoy Extraordinary from the Emperor, and one person with him; then another of the Duke's coaches with more of his gentlemen. Then another of the German Ambassador's coaches with more of his family in it. The Duke's pages walked by his coach, and had gold chains across their shoulders. The Baron de Lesley's went in some of the before-named coaches.

On Monday the 26th, Don John of Austria came to Court to give the Empress joy, but the ceremony performed, returned immediately, the same day, to a retiring place his Highness had at Ocana, near Aranjuez, which famous seat of royal recreation, for a farewell, the Empress lay at night at, being in her way to Denia, where she was to embark. Don John, from Ocana accompanied her Imperial Majesty two or three days' journey.

On Tuesday the 27th, my husband, (invited there by the Master of the Ceremonies, and then to come in short mourning, with something of jewels,) gave to the Empress joy in his master's name, also to the Queen jointly sent; and then giving her daughter the hand. Sir Robert Southwell was admitted to accompany him in like manner, and perform the same function.

On Wednesday the 18/28th of April, her Imperial Majesty went from the palace to the Descalcas Reales, and from thence to the Atoche, from whence she began her journey for Vienna. Her passing through the town was in this manner.

First passed several persons of quality in their coaches, intermixed with others. Then the two Lieutenants of her Catholic Majesty's guards, on horseback; then the two Captains of the said guards, the Marquis de Salina, and the Marquis de Malpica, on horseback. Then a coach of respect, lined with cloth of gold, mixed with green. Then a litter of respect lined with the same stuff; then four trumpeters on horseback; then the Duke of Albuquerque, in a plain coach; then twenty-four men upon horses and mules, with portmanteaus before them; then two trumpeters more; then the Empress and her Camarera Mayor (Condessa de Benavente), in a plain large coach; then eight men without cloaks on horseback, who I presume were pages to her Catholic Majesty; then the Empress's nurse, and four or five pretty children of her's in a coach; then four young ladies with caps and white feathers with black specks in them, in another coach; then duenas or ancient ladies; then more young ladies with caps and black hats, pinned up with rich jewels; then another coach with young ladies; then followed many other coaches irregularly.

The Duke de Medina de las Torres, as also the German Ambassador, and many of the nobility of Spain, went out of town, and stayed about a league off for the Empress's coming that way. All the meaner sort of her Imperial Majesty's train, and her carriages, as also the Duke of Albuquerque's, went before.

On Monday the 26th, I wrote to the Camarera Mayor and the Empress's Aya, giving both their Majesties joy of this marriage.

May the 5th, we dined at Salvatierra, two leagues from Madrid, and returned again at night.

On Friday the 18/28th of May, 1666, came to Madrid the Earl of Sandwich, Ambassador Extraordinary from our King to the Queen Regent of this kingdom. My husband went with all his train two leagues to welcome and conduct him to this Court. This day twenty-two years we were married.

The 29th, my Lord of Sandwich delivered my husband the King's letters of revocation, and therewith a private letter of great grace and favour. This afternoon my Lord Sandwich, with most part of his train, came to visit me.

June the 9th, stilo novo, being the King's birthday, my husband made an entertainment for my Lord of Sandwich., with all his retinue and the rest of the English at Madrid.

The next [Sun-] day, being Whit-Sunday, [Footnote: This was the last time my husband received the communion.] my husband went with the Earl of Sandwich to a private audience, where my husband introduced him to the King of Spain. Monday the 14th, my husband went with the Earl of Sandwich to the Duke de Medina de las Torres.

On the 15/25th, being Tuesday, [Footnote: Query, 5/15th June.] my husband was taken ill with an ague, but turned to a malignant inward fever, of which he lay until the 26th of the same month, being Sunday, [Footnote: Query, Saturday, 16/26th June.] until eleven of the clock at night, and then departed this life, fifteen days before his intended journey to England.

'O all powerful good God, look down from Heaven upon the most distressed wretch upon earth. See me with my soul divided, my glory and my guide taken from me, and in him all my comfort in this life; see me staggering in my path, which made me expect a temporal blessing for a reward of the great integrity, innocence, and uprightness of his whole life, and his patience in suffering the insolency of wicked men, whom he had to converse with upon the public employment, which thou thoughtest fit, in thy wisdom, to exercise him in. Have pity on me, O Lord, and speak peace to my disquieted soul, now sinking under this great weight, which, without thy support, cannot sustain itself. See me, O Lord, with five children, a distressed family, the temptation of the change of my religion, the want of all my friends, without counsel, out of my country, without any means to return with my sad family to our own country, now in war with most part of Christendom. But, above all, my sins, O Lord, I do lament with shame and confusion, believing it is for them that I receive this great punishment. Thou hast showed me many judgments and mercies which did not reclaim me, nor turn me to thy holy conversation, which the example of our blessed Saviour taught. Lord, pardon me; O God, forgive whatsoever is amiss in me; break not a bruised reed. I humbly submit to thy justice; I confess my wretchedness, and know I have deserved not only this but everlasting punishment; but, O my God, look upon me through the merits of my Saviour, and for his sake save me: do with me and for me what thou pleasest, for I do wholly rely on thy mercy, beseeching thee to remember thy promises to the fatherless and widow, and enable me to fulfil thy will cheerfully in this world; humbly beseeching thee that, when this mortal life is ended, I may be joined with the soul of my dear husband, and all thy servants departed this life in thy faith and fear, in everlasting praises of thy Holy Name. Amen.'

The next day my husband was embalmed. The following day I began to receive messages from the Queen and the Court of Spain.

July the 4th, stilo novo, 1666, my husband was buried by his own Chaplain, with the ceremony of the Church of England, and a sermon preached by him. In the evening I sent the body of my dear husband to Bilbao, intending suddenly to follow him: he went out of town privately, being accompanied only by a part of his own retinue. His body arrived safe at Bilbao on the 14th of July 1666, and was laid in the King's house. Mr. Cooper, Gentleman of his Horse; Mr. Jemett, who waited on him in his bed-chamber; Mr. Rookes, Mr. Weeden, Mr. Carew, Richard Batha, and Francis.

The 5th of July 1666, stilo novo, the Queen-Mother sent the Master of the Ceremonies of Spain to invite me to stay with all my children in her Court, promising me a pension of thirty thousand ducats a year, and to provide for my children, if I and they would turn our religion and become Roman Catholics. I answered, I humbly thanked her Majesty for her great grace and favour, which I would ever esteem and pay with my services, as far as I was able, all the days of my life; for the latter I desired her Majesty to believe that I could not quit the faith in which I had been born and bred, and in which God had pleased to try me for many years in the greatest troubles our nation hath ever seen; and that I do believe and hope that in the profession of my own religion God would hear my prayers, and reward her Majesty, and all the princes of that royal family, for this so great favour which her Majesty was pleased to offer me in my greatest affliction.

The 6th and 7th days of this month I was visited by the German Ambassador's lady, and several other ladies; also by the Ambassador and the Duke de Medina de las Torres, de Aveiro, Marquis de Trucifal, Conde de Monterey, with several others of that Court.

The Queen sent me, for a present, two thousand pistoles which her Majesty sent me word was to buy my husband a jewel if he had lived. The week following I gave the Secretary of State a gold watch and chain, worth thirty pounds. I gave the Master of the Ceremonies, at my coming away, a clock, which cost me forty pounds. I sold all my coaches and horses, and lumber of the house, to the Earl of Sandwich, for one thousand three hundred and eighty pistoles. I likewise sold there one thousand pounds' worth of plate to several persons, all the money I could make being little enough for my most sad journey to England.

The 8th of July 1666, at night, I took my leave of Madrid, and of the Siete Chimineas, the house so beloved of my husband and me formerly. I carried with me all my jewels, and the best of my plate, and other precious rarities, all the rest being gone before to Bilbao, with part of my family. All the women went in litters, and the men on horseback. Myself, my son, and four daughters, one gentlewoman, one chambermaid, Mr. Fanshawe, my husband's Secretary; Mr. Price, the Chaplain; Mr. Bagshawe, Mr. Creyton, Mr. White, Mr. Hellowe, John Burton, William, the Cook; besides other Spanish attendants.

My Lord Sandwich came in the afternoon to accompany me out of town, which offer, though earnestly pressed by my Lord, as well as by other persons of quality, I refused, desiring to go out of that place as privately as I could possibly; and I may truly say, never any Ambassador's family came into Spain more gloriously, or went out so sad.

July the 21st, after a tedious journey, we arrived at Bilbao, to which place my dear husband's body came the 14th of this month, and was lodged in the King's house, with some of his servants to attend him; but I hired a house in the town during my stay there, in which I received several letters from Madrid, from England, and from Paris. The Queen-Mother was graciously pleased to procure me passes from the King of France, which I received the 21st of September, stilo novo, accompanied by a letter from my Lady Guilford, and several others of her Majesty's Court; likewise I did receive a pass from the Duke of Beaufort, then at Lixa.

October the 1st, I sent answers of letters to England, to my Lord Arlington, my brother Warwick, my father, and to several other persons. Here heard the sad news of the burning of London.

December the 3rd, being Sunday, I began my journey from Bilbao, with the body of my dear husband, all my children, and all my family but three, whom I left to come with my goods by sea. The 7th of October, we came to Bayonne, in France, having had a dangerous

70

passage between Spain and France. October the 9th, we began our journey from Bayonne towards Paris, where we arrived the 30th of October, being Saturday.

November the 2nd, the Queen-Mother sent my Lady Guilford to condole my loss, and welcome me to Paris: many of her Majesty's family, of their own accord, did the same. On the 26th, her Majesty sent Mr. Church, in one of her coaches, to convey me to Chaillot, a nunnery, where the Queen then was, who received me with great grace and favour, and promised me much kindness, when her Majesty returned to England. Her Majesty sent by me letters to the King, Queen, Duke and Duchess of York, with a box of writings for her Majesty's Secretary, Sir John Winter.

November the 11th, we began our journey towards Calais; and upon the 11th of November, old style, we embarked at Calais in a little French man-of-war, which carried me to the Tower Wharf, where I landed the next day, at night, being Monday, at twelve of the clock. I made a little stay with my children at my father's house, on Tower-hill. The next day, being the 13th, we all went to my own house in Lincoln's-inn Fields, on the north side, where the widow Countess of Middlesex had lived before; and the same day, likewise, was brought the body of my dear husband.

On Saturday following, being the 16th of November 1666, I sent the body of my dear husband to be laid in my father's vault in Allhallows Church, in Hertford: none accompanied the hearse but seven of his own gentlemen, who had taken care of his body all the way from Madrid to London; being Mr. Fanshawe, Mr. Bagshawe, Mr. Cooper, Mr. Freyer, Mr. Creyton, Mr. Tarret, and Mr. Rooks.

On the 18th, my Lord Arlington visited me, proffering me his friendship, to be shown in the procuring of arrears of my husband's pay, which was two thousand pounds, and to reimburse me five thousand eight hundred and fifteen pounds my husband had laid out in his Majesty's service. Likewise I was visited to welcome me into England, and to condole my loss, by very many of the nobility and gentry, and also by all my relations in these parts.

November the 23rd, I waited on the King, and delivered to his Majesty my whole accounts. He was pleased to receive me very graciously, and promised me they should be paid, and likewise that his Majesty would take care of me and mine. Then I delivered his Majesty the letters I brought from the Queen-Mother; then I did my duty to the Queen, who with great sense condoled my loss, after which I delivered the Queen-Mother's letter sent to her Majesty by me. After staying two hours longer in her Majesty's bed-chamber, I waited on his Royal Highness, who having condoled me on the loss of my dear husband, promised me a ship to send for my goods and servants to Bilbao; then I waited on the Duchess, who with great grace and favour received me, and having been with her Highness about an hour, and delivered a letter from the Queen-Mother, I took my leave. I presented the King, Queen, Duke of York, and Duke of Cambridge, with two dozen of amber skins, and six dozen of gloves. I likewise presented my Lord Arlington with amber skins, gloves and chocolate, and a great picture, a copy of Titian's, to the value of one hundred pounds; and I made presents to Sir William Coventry, and several other persons then in office.

In February, the Duke ordered me the Victory frigate, to bring the remainder of my goods and people from Bilbao, in Spain, which safely arrived in the latter end of March 1667. I spent my time much in soliciting and petitioning my Lord Treasurer Southampton, for the present dispatch of my accounts, which did pass the Secretary, then Lord Arlington, and within two months I got a privy seal for my money, without either fee or present, which I could never fasten on my Lord. Now I thought myself happy, and feared nothing less than further trouble. God, that only knows what is to come, so disposed my fortune, that losing that good man and friend, Lord Southampton, my money, which was five thousand six hundred pounds, was not paid me until December 1669, notwithstanding I had tallies for the money above two years before. This was above two thousand pounds loss to me. Besides, these commissioners, by the instigation of one of their fellow commissioners, my Lord Shaftesbury, the worst of men, persuaded them that I might pay for the Embassy plate, which I did, two thousand pounds; and so maliciously did he oppress me, as if he hoped in me to destroy that whole stock of honesty and innocence which he mortally hates. In this great distress I had no remedy but patience: how far that was from a reward, judge ye, for near thirty years' suffering by land and sea, and the hazard of our lives over and over, with the many services of your father, and the expense of all the monies we could procure, and seven years' imprisonment, with the death and beggary of many eminent persons of our family, who when they first entered the King's service, had great and clear estates. Add to this the careful management of the King's honour in the Spanish Court, after my husband's death, which I thought myself bound to maintain, although I had not, God is my witness, above twenty-five doubloons by me at my husband's death, to bring home a family of three score servants, but was forced to sell one thousand pounds' worth of our own plate, and to spend the Queen's present of two thousand doubloons in my journey to England, not owing nor leaving one shilling debt in Spain, I thank God, nor did my husband leave any debt at home, which every Ambassador cannot say. Neither did these circumstances following prevail to mend my condition, much less found I that compassion I expected upon the view of myself, that had lost at once my husband, and fortune in him, with my son but twelve months old in my arms, four daughters, the eldest but thirteen years of age, with the body of my dear husband daily in my sight for near six months together, and a distressed family, all to be by me in honour and honesty provided for, and to add to my afflictions, neither persons sent to conduct me, nor pass, nor ship, nor money to carry me one thousand miles, but some few letters of compliment from the chief ministers, bidding, 'God help me!' as they do to beggars, and they might have added, 'they had nothing for me,' with great truth. But God did hear, and see, and help me, and brought my soul out of trouble; and by his blessed providence, I and you live, move, and have our being, and I humbly pray God that that blessed providence may ever supply our wants. Amen.

Seeing what I had to trust to, I began to shape my life as well as I could to my fortune, in order whereunto I dismissed all my family but some few persons. At my arrival I gave them all mourning, and five pounds apiece, and put most of them into a good way of living, I thank God.

In 1667, I took a house in Holborn-row, Lincoln's-inn Fields, for twenty-one years, of Mr. Cole. This year I christened a daughter of Lord Fanshawe's. Here, in this year, I only spent my time in lament and dear remembrances of my past happiness and fortune; and though I had great graces and favours from the King and Queen, and whole Court, yet I found at the present no remedy. I often reflected how many miscarriages and errors the fall from that happy estate I had been in would throw me; and as it is hard for the rider to quit his horse in a full career, so I found myself at a loss, that hindered my settling myself in a narrow compass suddenly, though my narrow fortune required it; but I resolved to hold me fast by God, until I could digest, in some measure, my afflictions. Sometimes I thought to quit the world as a sacrifice to your father's memory, and to shut myself up in a house for ever from all people; but upon the consideration of my children, who were all young and unprovided for, being wholly left to my care and disposal, I resolved to suffer, as long as it pleased God, the storms and flows of fortune.

As soon as I got my tallies placed again by the Commissioners, I sold them for five hundred pounds less than my assignments to Alderman Buckwell, who gave me ready money, and I put it out upon a mortgage of Sir Richard Ayloff's estate, in Essex, at Braxted.

In 1668, I hired a house and ground, of sixty pounds a year, at Hartingfordbury, in Hertfordshire, to be near my father, being but two miles from Balls, both because I would have my father's company, and because the air was very good for my children; but when God took my father, I let my time in it, and never saw it more.

About this time Sir Philip Warwick retired himself from public business, to his house at Frogpool, in Kent; his son and daughter-in-law lived with him some time, until this year, 1669, they went into France. She was the daughter and coheir of the Lord Freschville.

In my brother Warwick's house, in London, in 1666, died my sister Bedell, and was carried down into Huntingdonshire, to Hamerton, and was there buried by her husband in the chancel. She was a most worthy woman, and eminently good, wise, and handsome; she never much enjoyed herself since the death of her eldest daughter, who married Sir Francis Compton, and, in her right, he had Hamerton, in Huntingdonshire. She died five years before my sister, a most dutiful daughter, and a very fine-bred lady, and excellent company, and very virtuous.

About this time died my brother Lord Fanshawe's widow. She was a very good wife and tender mother, but else nothing extraordinary. She was buried in the vault of her husband's family in Ware church. Within a year after this, his son, Lord Fanshawe, sold Ware Park for 26,000 pounds to Sir Thomas Byde, a brewer, of London.

Thus, in the fourth generation, the chief of our family, since they came into the south, for their sufferings for the Crown, sold the flower of their estates, and near 2000 pounds a year more. There remains but the Remembrancer's place of the Exchequer office: and very pathetical is the motto of our arms for us—'The victory is in the Cross.' [Footnote: "In Cruce Victoria." Another motto of the Fanshawe family was, "Dux vitae ratio." Of these mottoes a Correspondent in the Gentleman's Magazine for July 1796, tells the following story. "When Sir Richard was ambassador, and was travelling in Spain, in an English carriage, with his arms upon it, surrounded by the two mottoes belonging to them—Dux vitae Ratio—In Cruce Victoria; a crowd of peasants gathering round the unusual sight of so many foreigners, in a town where they stopped for refreshment, were very anxious with a priest, who happened to be amongst them, for an explanation of the Latin, which being beyond his skill, he informed them that the coach belonged to the Duke of Vitae Ratio, who had done great things for the Cross."]

I had, about this time, some trouble with keeping the lordships of Tring and Hitching, which your father held of the Queen-Mother; but I not being able to make a considerable advantage of them, gave them up again: and then I sold a lease of the Manor of Burstalgarth, which was granted for thirty-one years to your father from the King. Dean Hicks bought it, it being convenient for him, lying upon Humber. There was a widow, one Mrs. Hiliard, hired this manor, and had so done long. She was very earnest to buy it at a very under rate. When she saw it sold, she, as was suspected, fired the house, which was burnt down to the ground within two months after I had sold it.

In this year my brother Harrison married the eldest daughter of the Lord Viscount Grandison. I let in this year a lease of eleven years of Fanton Hall, in Essex, to Jonathan Wier, which I held of the Bishopric of London: this lease was bought the first year the King came home, of Doctor Sheldon, then Bishop of London, who was exceeding kind to us, and sold it for half the worth, which I will ever acknowledge with thankfulness.

My dear father departed this life, upon the 28th of September, 1670, being above eighty years of age, in perfect understanding, God be praised! He left five hundred pounds to every one of my four daughters; and gave me three thousand pounds for a part of the manor of Scallshow, near Lynn, in Norfolk, but the year before he died, to make my sister Harrison a jointure. The 11th I christened the eldest daughter of my brother Harrison, with Lord Grandison, and Sir Edmund Turner.

The death of my father made so great an impression on me, that with the grief, I was sick half a year almost to death; but through God's mercy, and the care of Doctor Jasper Needham, a most worthy and learned physician, I recovered; and as soon as I was able to think of business, I bought ground in St. Mary's Chapel, in Ware Church, of the Bishop of London, and there made a vault for my husband's body, which I had there laid by most of the same persons that laid him before in my father's vault, in Hertford Church deposited, until I could make this vault and monument, which cost me two hundred pounds; and here, if God pleases, I intend to lie myself.

He had the good fortune to be the first chosen, and the first returned member of the Commons' House of Parliament, in England, after the King came home; and this cost him no more than a letter of thanks, and two brace of bucks, and twenty broad pieces of gold to buy them wine. Upon St. Stephen's day the King shut the

EXTRACTS
FROM THE
CORRESPONDENCE
OF
SIR RICHARD FANSHAWE
ILLUSTRATIVE OF THE MEMOIR

The Letters from which part of the following Extracts have been taken, were printed in 1701, under the title of "Original Letters of his Excellency Sir Richard Fanshawe, during his Embassies in Spain and Portugal; which, together with divers Letters and Answers from the Chief Ministers of State of England, Spain, and Portugal, contain the whole negociations of the treaty of Peace between those three Crowns." 8vo, pp. 510.

The remainder are now printed, for the first time, from the rough copies of the originals, or the originals themselves, preserved in the Harleian MS. 7010, in the British Museum.

Although these Extracts were chiefly made with the view of illustrating the statements in the Memoir, nearly every passage has been copied from the Correspondence which is of the slightest general interest, unconnected with political affairs.

To MR. SECRETARY BENNET.

[See MEMOIRS, p 152.]

On Board his Majesty's Admiral, entering the Bay of Cadiz, Wednesday about noon, 24th of February, 1669, English style.

"By former advertisements, I presume his Majesty, from you, hath understood how, after sharp storms and cross winds, with the first favourable breath we adventured to put to sea a third time, and out of Torbay the second, upon Monday the 15th instant, at nine of the clock at night; from whence in so few days, as appears by computation, to the time of the date hereof, and with the most auspicious weather that could be imagined, we were all arrived thus far, in perfect health and safety; where perceiving some sailors steering towards us, which we took to be English, and homewards bound, I thought it my duty, en duda, to prepare hastily, thus much only, against we speak with them in passage; which may suffice at present, from him who knows no more as yet."

Original Letters of Sir Richard Fanshawe, p. 30.

To MR. SECRETARY BENNET.

[See MEMOIRS, p. 153.]

Cadiz, February 29, 1663/March 10, 1664.

My last of the 29th of February, English style, (which yet cannot go sooner than this, having not met with the present opportunity of conveyance I then expected,) advertised your honour we were just then entering this bay, after a brief and very fair passage from Torbay.

The same evening we came to anchor at some distance from this city, intending, God willing, the next day, 6th instant, to come on shore; but a strong Levant rising, not only that was impossible, but even for any to come to me from the land.

The next morning, 7th, our ships weighing, made a hard shift to get into the port, and I from thence a harder to land in boats. The Duke of Medina Celi, in the interim, having complimented me aboard, by a Caballero de el Habito, with a letter from Port S. Mary, and in person from this city the deputed governor of this town, Don Diego de Ibarra, both of them, as by a general order from his Catholic Majesty, which they had had some weeks by them in case of my arrival here, in virtue whereof somewhat more than ordinary salutes were given by this city to his Majesty's Ambassador and fleet; also a house ready furnished for me, whereunto I was very honourably conducted, with appearance of universal joy, and there visited the same day by the Duke of Albuquerque, the Cabildo, and all the nobles and principal gentlemen here residing. My table, the governor signified, was to be at my own finding, yet that I must not refuse to accept of the first meal from him; of the former I was very glad, as enjoying thereby a liberty which I preferred to any delicacies whatsoever upon free cost; the latter, I was not at all nice to receive for once. But I had not been three hours on shore, when an Extraordinary arrived from Madrid, with more particular orders than formerly from his Catholic Majesty, importing, that our Master's fleet, when arrived, and this Ambassador, should be presaluted from the city, in a manner unexampled to others, and which should not be drawn into example hereafter. Moreover, and this so likewise, that I and all my company must be totally defrayed, both here and all the way up to Madrid, upon his Catholic Majesty's account; with several other circumstances of particular esteem for our Royal Master above all the world besides. The substance of all hath been related to me, and the effects declare it; but a copy of the order itself I have not as yet been able to obtain though desired, it being the style not to communicate it without leave from above, and out of the Secretary of State, else I should have thought it my duty to remit it unto his Majesty from hence, and shall from thence if I get it.

The first night the keys of the city were brought to me in a great silver basin, by the governor, which, after several refusals, I took and put into the right hands; then the governor forced me to give him the word, which, after like refusals, I did, and was Viva el Rey Catolico.

At supper, he and his Lady would bear me and my wife company, which I accepting as a great favour, told him my wife should eat with her Ladyship, retired from the men, after the Spanish fashion, it being more than sufficient, they would not think strange, we used the innocent freedom of our own when we were among ourselves. But by no means, that he would not suffer; and to keep us the more in countenance, alleged this manner of eating to be now the custom of many of the greatest families of Spain, and had been from all antiquity to this day of the majestical House of Alva; the generosity whereof, particularly in the person of the present duke, he took this occasion to celebrate very highly. So, in fine, he had his will of me in this particular.

As the Duke of Albuquerque, newly created Generalissimo of the Ocean, and very shortly going to enjoy that high puesto at his ease in the Court, where he is likewise Gentilhombre de la Camara—had done to me before, so yesterday his Duchess and their daughter, (married to his own brother, to keep up the name, for want of issue male,) both vastly rich in jewels, as lately returned from the viceroyship of Mexico, so full as to refuse that of Peru, in consequence of the other, began an obliging visit of many hours to my wife; both of the above-named Dukes and Duchess, whether by letter and message, as the Duke of Medina, or in person, as the other, treating us both to a full equality in all respects.

I had forgot to specify, as I may have done several other remarkable points of respect to his Majesty's Ambassador, how one part of this King's last order was, that for more honour and security, a guard of soldiers, with a captain of it, should be night and day in my house; which is practised where I now am, and, as I understood it, is to be in like manner in all towns of note; a person of quality, by the same royal command, conducting me from one to another.

All this ceremony, I hope, is not instead of substance; for then it would prove very tedious and irksome to me indeed; but an earnest and prognostic of it, which time will try when I come to treat.—Ibid. p. 31.

To MR. SECRETARY BENNET.

[See MEMOIRS, pp. 159-166.]

Seville, March 23, 1663, 2 April, 1664

Pursuing my journal, from the date of my last to you from Cadiz, Feb. 29th, 1663/March 10th, 1664 you may be pleased to understand that, March 3/13, the old Governor, D. Ant. Pimentel, returned thither, surprising me with a visit in my house before he would enter into his own, or had any notice of his landing; the cause of his suspension having been only that which I then signified, and as powerfully removed at Court by a letter from the Duke de Medina Celi to his Catholic Majesty in his defence, as it seemed to have been laid on with a very good will by the Duke of Albuquerque; the letter I have seen, wanting neither rhetoric, logic, nor assurance.

6/16, (of the same.) The said Don Antonio treated me and all my company with splendour and magnificence, borrowing us for that dinner from the King's entertainment.

The 9/19. Himself in person accompanied me to Port St. Mary, my first step towards Madrid, and had been my first landing-place, as nearest and of most convenience, if it had not been signified to me by message, that I must not waive Cadiz, where all things were orderly prepared for my reception, from whence also I pressed to have removed sooner; but that the Duke of Medina intimated his desire of the contrary, as not till then so well prepared for my entertainment as his Excellency intended to be; and in particular, because a rich gondola, built purposely, said they, for the wafting over of Princes, had some days' work to do about it, before it could be fitted for my transportation.

Arrived therein at Port St. Mary, the Duke, with all his family and vassals, (that city being his patrimony,) met me at the landing-place, whence, with coaches, and vollies of shot by many troops, not upon the King's pay but his own, for so his Excellency then told me, he conducted me to a very fair house, prepared by his care, and furnished with the richest of what he had for his own palace moreover, under his Excellency's proper inspection against my coming from Cadiz, whence, having been there revisited at parting by the Duke of Albuquerque, and all other who had visited me at my arrival, I was dismissed with great and small shot from the town, and in like manner saluted in my passage by the Spanish Armada, and all other ships in the bay, as well Spanish as strangers, Van Tromp riding there at the same time with his squadron. The rest of my entertainment at Port St. Mary was proportionable to the beginning, and there also the Duke of Medina gave me one treat at his own palace. The civilities to me of the Marquis of Bayona, Gentleman of the Galleys of Spain, the constant station thereof is there, and of his lady to my wife, inheritrix or the Marquisate of Santa Cruz, and so of a Grandeeship, noted likewise for eminent virtue and education at Court, came nothing behind; but these two great men cannot set their horses together.

On Monday, March 14/24, I was accompanied out of the city of Port by the Duke of Medina, Don Antonio de Pimentel, who had never left me till then, being one, and the Marquis of Bayona, with his Lady, planting his coach upon the way-side, beyond the place where the Duke took leave. I came that night to Xerez de la Frontera; met and welcomed before our approaching to the city by the magistrates thereof and principal gentlemen, that is all, with many troops of soldiers, and shoals of common people. The next day, treated in the interim, and then dismissed as before at the other two places, I arrived and lodged at Lebrija. The next at Utrera; met about a league short, by order of the Conde de Molina, Assistente de Sevilla, with a troop of horse, and by Don Lope de Mendoza, Alguazil, mayor of the city, as Teniente del Duque de Alcal, proprietor by inheritance of that office, the said Don Lope being, by the same order, to conduct me as far as Cordova.

The next day, 16/26 of March, accompanied with the same troop and conductor, we set forth for Seville; but this small stream soon lost itself, when, about the distance before named it fell into a torrent of people of all sorts and degrees, both military and civil, which, together with the Conde Assistente, rushed out to receive and conduct me to the King's palace, or Alcazar, which accordingly was done. Churches, streets, inhabitants, river, places much noted at all times, setting now upon this occasion the best side outward to express a pride in their joy of a hoped perfect correspondence with England.

Here, at my arrival, I found lying for me, in the hand of a servant of the Duke of Medina de las Torres, a letter from his Excellency, of high welcome to Spain, and no less respect. Here, since my arrival, besides a perpetual court of company and entertainments of the best above stairs, and ranks of soldiers, with multitudes of others below, upon my account, in this famous palace of the King, where I am lodging in his Majesty's own bedchamber, as royally furnished as when himself was in it, visits I have received in form from their Excellency the City, by their Representatives; from their Senoria the Audiencia, by their Regente; from their Senoria the Contratacion House, by their Presidente; and from his Illustrissima the Archbishop, being at present sick, by message; all which I have repaid respectively; and tomorrow, God willing, set forth towards Cordova; perceiving beforehand that my salida will be proportionable to my entrada. The conclusion I make of the whole is, 'thus shall it be done to the man whom the King our Master is pleased to honour,' and the King of Spain, for his Majesty's sake, as far as outward ceremony can testify it; well, hoping that neither his Majesty, nor any other at home, will apprehend I take aught of this as done to my person, or for any thing of intrinsic value supposed to be in me, but merely as I bear my master's image and superscription; his Majesty's prerogative shining the more therein, by how much the metal on which he is stamped hath less of value in itself. Not a compliment, which will be always a saucy thing, as well as impertinent, with a man's prince; but a sober and natural inference, at least so understood by such as could wish it were otherwise.—Ibid. p. 36.

To MR. SECRETARY BENNET.
[See MEMOIRS, pp. 167, 168.]
Cordova, 29 March/7 April, 1664.

My last journal—such I call all letters of mine as related only to my motions towards Madrid—with something of the splendid and ceremonious entertainment of his Majesty's

Ambassador, from place to place, more or less as the places themselves are more or less eminent and plentiful, was dated at Seville, 23 Mart, 1663/2 Aprilis, 1664 and figured *l*.

The next day, according to the account I then made, departed from Seville, accompanied out of the city about a mile by the Conde Assistente, and divers other of the nobility and gentry of that place, and was guarded by foot soldiers quite through the city, with colours displayed, and abased as I passed by, and muskets discharged; a company of foot having been upon my guard all the while I stayed there, as in all other places of note.

That night I came to Carmona, a city formerly considerable for the lofty situation, strong, and pleasant palace there of the Kings of Castile, and were the last which held out for Don Pedro the Cruel; both the one and the other now ruinous enough. About half a league short thereof, I was met by the magistrates and gentry of the place, and by them conducted to my lodging; having placed a company of foot at the entrance into the town, who discharged their muskets, &c.

From Carmona, the next day, to Fuentes; a very pleasant and healthful small town, from whence the Marquis, uncle to the now Duke Medina Sidonia, had his title. From Fuentes, the next day, to Ezija; which, in respect of the great heats thereof at some times, is called 'the Frying-pan of Andaluzia,' yet we, upon the 5th of April, their style, found it cold enough. I was there very civilly and splendidly lodged and entertained for two days; being, indeed, an extraordinary place. Our company and cattle harassed; and foreseeing we must make a halt at Cordova till the Holy Week, now begun, were past, and therefore to no purpose to hurry thither.

From Ezija, 28 March/7th April, I arrived at Cordova, where now I am: where also my reception without this most ancient and famous city, by the Corregidor and gentry thereof, the flower of all Spain for extraction and civility, was, and our lodging and treatment of all sorts within is, and is like to be, do what we can, and the Lent season too, to avoid and qualify it, such as will require a letter apart, and more lines therein, to abbreviate it only, than the feasting and pastimes themselves will probably allow me leisure for whilst I am here; and therefore I must defer that to another occasion.—Ibid. p. 44.

To MR. SECRETARY BENNET
[See MEMOIRS, pp. 168-170.]
Ballecas, one league from Madrid, 7th May, 1664, stilo loci.

My last from Cordova, 29th of March, N. S. 7th of April, carried on the journal of my great reception and entertainment in my way up to Madrid, to the day of the date thereof.

What was afterwards in the same city, whilst I remained there, which was until Tuesday in Easter Week—because those gentlemen would needs make the King of England's Ambassador a fiesta of canas upon the Monday, at the rate of taking up their horses from verde, [Footnote: i.e., From grass.] on purpose for it; and since, in all other places proportionably, particularly in Toledo, where there was another fiesta of bulls given, was every way rather exceeding than inferior to any thing that was elsewhere before, until my safe arrival at this very place, which I reckon my journey's end; and by earnest suit to this Court from Seville, did obtain it might be so esteemed by them; leaving me here to my own expense and disposal, although I have as yet no house provided for me in Madrid; notwithstanding all diligence towards it by the Aposentadores there, upon the King's special command, and also by such private persons as I myself have employed not to stick at any just rate for a good one, upon my particular account, with advance of a year's rent in plata doble, and so to be continued, as long as the house should be used by me, upon merchant security: such a dearth there is really of accommodations of this nature for the present, and for a long time hath been; yet there want not descants, that there is some great mystery of state in the matter, which doubtless will fly as far as Paris, if not reach London.

POSTSCRIPT.—Since my arrival in this village, and that my present want of a house in Madrid is more murmured at there than needs, considering the King is absent, and moreover, though I am much straitened in matter of lodgings, yet that I have a very large and pleasant garden thereunto belonging, to expatiate and refresh myself and wearied family in, I received a message from Baron Battevil to this effect, besides general tenders of all manner of service which is in his power; that he is at present (as in truth he is) sick, or else would have waited upon me himself in person; but that he will with all his heart quit his house to me—which I am told is a very fine one, as he hath made it, with chargeable additions of his own, in the midst of the Calle de Alcala, with a fair garden to it, and that it is no compliment at all. This I have thought reasonable to advertise in England, though not to accept.—Ibid. p.63-66.

FROM THE DUKE DE MEDINA DE LAS TORRES, TO SIR RICHARD FANSHAWE.

Madrid, 27th of May, 1664.

"The Bull-feast will be on Thursday next; and by reason that your Excellency seems desirous to be a spectator incognito, I have taken care to procure you a shady balcony in the first story. I have likewise ordered a window to be secured for your Excellency's retinue. If there be anything more wherein I can serve your Excellency, I hope you will freely command it, as I shall be always forward to serve you. God keep your Excellency, and grant you the long life I desire."— Ibid. p. 86.

To MR. SECRETARY BENNET.

Ballecas, 18/28 May, 1664.

The Duke of Aveiro had recovered, by final sentence, the 17th of May, the two dukedoms of Maqueda and Najara. Maqueda he hath; for Najara he hath not yet sued, but keeps it in the decks: then Maqueda is a great deal better worth than I thought, valued by some at sixty thousand ducats per annum, at forty thousand generally; and moreover his sister, (as a domestic, who you know, of that family, tells me,) as a consequent of the late sentence, will recover for, or towards, her dowry, a deposited arrear of between three or four hundred thousand ducats. She was lately, in all appearance, very near marriage with the heir of the Conde de Oropesa; but quite broke off before this sentence, upon point of alimony, and liberty of rewarding her own attendants out of her own estate, in case of future dissension. I am particular in the domestic concernments of this family when they come in my way, though the passages relate nothing of interest of state, in regard to that esteem or their persons, [Footnote: The following passage occurs in Sir Richard's instructions: "You shall visit, in our name, the Duke of Aveiro and his sister, assuring them of our friendship and particular concernments for their persons, for the name and royal blood of which they are descended, and promising them all effects of it in our power, especially if the agreement between the two Crowns give us an opportunity to have any part in the restitution of their estates, with all other good offices, which shall happen to be in our power."—Ibid. p. 17.] which his Majesty's instruction to me on that behalf doth express, and knowing yourself to be particularly an honourer of them.

Upon the 22nd current, Ascension-day at night, [Footnote: In 1664 Ascension-day fell on the NINETEENTH of May] after a play in the palace, upon a slight occasion of snappish words, unless there were something of old grudge or rivalship in the case, the Marquis of Albersan, challenging Don Domingo Guzman, and he fought under the palace, near the Marquis de Castel Rodrigo's house in the Florida, where Don Domingo gave the Marquis that whereof he died. The next morning they that knew the Marquis to be so near and dear to the Conde de Castrillo as he was, and knew Don Domingo to be the Duke of St. Lucar's son, knowing withal how well that Conde and Duke do love one another, and how they do both divide the Spanish world between them in power, will conclude this private accident hath an influence upon the public; indeed so great a one, as hath seemed for some days past to make a vacation in Court, that I may not call it an inter-reign, or the dividing of a kingdom against itself.

For since, and upon, this accident, all seems of a light flame between these duumviri, to so high a degree, that each crossing whatsoever the other promotes, the most of others of quality take sides, and such as appear neuters with the monarchy a monopoly in either of their hands; weeping over the graves of the Conde, Duque, and Don Luis de Haro, because they were absolute and sole favourites in their generations; attributing to this very cause the seeming disproportion, if not contradiction, between my reception in, and conduction from, Cadiz, hitherto, and now my long demurrage so near the Court, for want of a house in it, and prophesying already that this animosity and emulation will gangrene into the substance, as well as accidents, of my embassy.

I do not here pretend to paint unto his Majesty the state of Spain, but the populace of it; asking more time, by a great number of years, to understand the former, though but in a competent measure, than I hope his Majesty will give me: and if his Majesty would, God will not. I have learned by the yet invincible ignorance of some Foreign Ambassadors to England (an open-breasted country!—how apt they are to mistake), who (begging the question, in the first place, of their own personal abilities) can never be convinced that Mas vee el loco en su casa, que el cuerdo en la agena.—Whilst I am writing, I am called to entertain the Count de Marcin, [Footnote: John Gasper Ferdinand de Marcin, Count de Graville, Marquis de Claremont d'Antrague, &c., Captain-General of the Spanish Service, was Lieutenant-General of Charles the Second's forces by sea and land, and was elected a Knight of the Garter in 1658.] who is upon the way from Madrid to find me out in this obscurity, contrary to the style of Spain, but suitable to the freedom of a soldier, and of a subject of his Majesty, as to his most noble Sovereignty of the Garter.—Ibid. p. 90.

TO HIS EXCELLENCY DENZILL LORD HOLLES, AMBASSADOR EXTRAORDINARY IN THE COURT OF FRANCE. FOR HIS MAJESTY'S SPECIAL SERVICE.

[See MEMOIRS, pp. 170, 171]

Madrid, June 10/20, 1664.

MY LORD,

After a long progress from Cadiz to Ballecas, a village one league distant from this Court, and almost as long a parenthesis there—which the French Court will say was no elegant piece of oratory, nor the middle at all proportionable to the beginning with me, whatever the end may prove—upon the 8th instant I arrived happily at my journey's end howsoever; where, as speedily then as myself could possibly in any measure be ready for it, namely, upon the 18th, both stilo loci, I received my public audience of entrada at the King's palace, in the same form, neither more or less, as my predecessors have ever done; and only two days having since intervened, as by the account doth appear, within two or three more from the date of this, the King removing to-day unto the Buen Retiro, I do expect my first private audience.

Being thus fixed, after long running, in the centre of my negotiation, I do presume to beg from your Excellency, and hereby to begin on my part, a mutual correspondence; first in order to the service of our Royal master, whereunto we are both obliged in common; secondly, to that of your Excellency, whereunto myself in particular.

To begin with what concerns my embassy, being so much a fresh man as your Excellency sees I am in this Court, visible it is by what proceeds, I can as yet have nothing to descant or touch upon, but matter of ceremony only from and towards me, divisible into two considerations; the first, in reference to the past, of which I have already said the same hath been, as from, and to, other Ambassadors, in all this and all other ages; the second, in reference to the present concurring Ambassadors, and other public ministers of this Court; and now upon this branch I shall, with your Excellency's patience, if I may presume so much, dilate myself so far as to the heads only of what hath past, in fact, as followeth.

I need not tell your Excellency, because it differs not from the custom of all or most Courts, until abuses thereof enforced an alteration in some, that in this, always heretofore, Ambassadors and other Foreign Ministers upon the place, did send their families to accompany new comers to their first public audience, and this went round. Therefore, accordingly, I was now, in my turn, to expect this function towards me, as I did. The Master of the Ceremonies thereupon, who is a man new in his place, advertised me in writing, that this, since Henry the Eighth's time, was never practised to, nor by, Ambassadors of England. Finding this matter of fact utterly mistaken, I replied. Soon after he brought me a message from the King, that I should not expect this ceremony; but still upon the same misgrounded supposition, therefore unto this likewise I replied. Finally, his Majesty, having weighed my last reply, by the Secretary of State for the North, Don Blasco de Loyola, coming to my house the evening before my audience, signified to me, that for certain reasons, whatsoever was heretofore in practice of that kind, it must thenceforward be no more, from or towards English, or any Ambassador whatsoever in this Court, the which being his Majesty's own order, in his own kingdom, and equally indifferent to all, my answer to the Secretary was—That for the present I saw no further cause of reply, but would and did submit thereunto.

The like signification was at the same time sent to all other Ambassadors and Foreign Ministers here that they would not send, the which, in compliance therewith, they forbear, all but the French, who upon the very morning, the hour of my audience approaching, sent four of his gentlemen, with one of his coaches, to accompany me. The Marquis de Malpica, mayor-domo of the week, and Captain of the German guard, in behalf of the Marquis of Salinas, proprietor thereof, happening to be my conductor, with his guard, did a little expostulate with those gentlemen, why they came contrary to his Majesty's order; who replied, their Lord did receive no orders but from his own master, who had sent him very strict ones to perform, I think he said this office in particular, at least, in general, all offices of amity to the Ambassador of the King of England, his Christian Majesty's most dear brother and ally. In fine, accompany me they did, and very civilly comported themselves, both unto the palace, which was customary, but now forbid, and home again, which was never done before, by the family of any Ambassador, to any other whatsoever in this Court. They did insist that their Ambassador's coach should precede my second coach, which was not denied them, being a civil expedient practised in all or most other courts; the ordinary style of this, and practised, by these individual French themselves towards public ministers of the lowest rank, as they avowed to me the same morning, in the presence both of the Marquis and the Master of Ceremonies, and expressly a majori, that whenever I should send in the like case to accompany a new comer from France, the same measure would never be scrupled towards me.

For this obliging piece of gallantry to the King of England's Ambassador, endeared by the singularity, by the opposition of the Spanish Court, and by the supererogation of his followers extending it in part beyond the example of others, when the same was in custom, I wrote my thanks yesterday unto his Excellency, who answered, that if he had not had the orders of the King his master to pay me the respects he did, it would have sufficed for obliging him thereunto, to know that the King of England's Mother is his Master's Aunt. My Lord, there are in this Court, who seem of opinion, that this excess of courtesy from the French Ambassador, is not sound within, looking one way and rowing another; which, say they, will shortly appear. For my own part, I am quite of another mind; and hitherto I am sure, in farther demonstrations of kindness and civility, he followeth suit with the forwardest, if in that he was the single unfollowed precedent. I am, my Lord, your Excellency's most faithful, and ever most obedient Servant, RICHARD FANSHAWE.—Ibid. p. 106.

To MR. SECRETARY BENNET.
[See MEMOIRS, p. 171 and p. 175.]
Madrid, Wednesday, the 15th June, 1664, English Style.
"I write this, being just now returned from my first private audience of his Catholic Majesty, which was given me in the Buen Retiro, and therein did deliver myself in the sense of my instructions and directions; not in many words, because the King's weak state of body will not allow it; but with much plainness and humble freedom, concerning the languishing and desperate condition in which the peace and commerce between the Crowns and nations have long lain gasping, and expecting an utter dissolution, by frequent violations of articles in several manners."—Ibid, p. 113.

Madrid, Wednesday, 25th June, 1664.
In the first place, having procured his Catholic Majesty to be prepared to expect it, I delivered myself in English, and in the express words of my instructions, only changing the person, as followeth, viz.

"The most Serene King of Great Britain, my Master, hath charged me, after kissing your Majesty's feet with due reverence, to represent unto your Catholic Majesty, that some unhappy accidents intervening, have occasioned his not performing this part towards your Majesty sooner, in return of those congratulatory embassies which your most Serene Majesty sent unto him immediately upon his late happy restoration to his kingdoms. His most Serene Majesty commanded me to add farther, that neither those accidents, nor any other, of what nature soever, have been, or can be able, to lessen his esteem of your royal person and friendship, or the obligations he had to your most Serene Majesty in the time of his adversity; and that therefore your Majesty may assure yourself, that his Majesty will be ready in all times to make proportionable returns.'

With this, and the delivering to his Catholic Majesty, first my Latin credential, then the respects of the whole Royal Family of England, in general words, and particularly a letter from his Royal Highness; also, his Majesty's leave first asked, presenting my comrades one after another to do their obeisance, I made my retreat in the accustomed manner.

The like respectively, immediately after, in the Queen's side, to her Majesty, unto whom I presented his Majesty's letter, and afterwards two others from their Royal Highnesses; then a compliment to the Empress, so treated as to title, but ranked as to place, because not yet espoused beneath the Queen her mother, and would have been also, (had his Highness been there present, as was intended, but that it proved either his sleeping or eating hour,) beneath her brother the Prince; all which seemed very graciously accepted; and here no English at all was spoken. Lastly, a dumb show of salute, as you know the custom to be, after the Queen and Empress, to every particular dame; and in the close of this ceremony, as well towards their Majesties as the ladies, my comrades had all of them leave to follow me.

The evening, and near that time it was before we had gotten home and eaten our breakfast, was wholly spent by me in expected visits to the Duke of Medina de las Torres, and the rest of the Council, the President of Castile (quatenus such) only excepted by me, as likewise by all other Ambassadors of the first class used to be. This is the reason why, for haste, having only a piece of the night for my own before the post departs, I write to you bare matter of fact in this misshapen way hitherto; and in another point, perhaps of more import in the consequence than all the rest, I must be forced, for the same reason, to go yet less, only touching thereupon very briefly for the present.

You well know a custom of this Court, and I believe of most others likewise, till abuses thereof enforced an alteration in some, that Ambassadors and other Foreign Ministers upon the place, send their families to accompany any new comers to their first public audience; and this went round, Accordingly, I was now to expect this function towards me, as I did.

[Sir Richard then repeats precisely what he stated in his Letter to Lord Holles.—See pages 254, 255]

So that hitherto, as to this action, they can have nothing to boast of, but an excess of civility towards the crown of England, or the person of our Royal Master. In return whereunto, his Majesty, in my humble opinion, will think fit to command me, or whosoever shall succeed me, to perform the same office towards the successor of this French Ambassador. As to both points, which make it worthy of peculiar estimation, that is to say, with an exception in this one particular only, though his Catholic Majesty should continue his present general rule to the contrary; and although also, even whilst his compliment was generally practised, it was not by any extended so far as to accompany any Ambassador back to his house; and this the rather, if it shall be found that the French Ambassador, conforming hereafter to the general rule, as to all others, shall have made the English Ambassador his single exception in the case. The experiment will now soon be made, a new Venetian Ambassador being daily expected here; though possibly he may not have his audience so very soon after, but that, in the interim, I may, upon this clear, though brief, stating of all actions and circumstances to me, as yet appear above ground in this matter, receive his Majesty's particular directions and cautions how to carry myself in all events, the which I am exceedingly desirous of; and, in default thereof, will, with all fidelity, proceed and work according to the best of my understanding.

If it be not already clear enough from the premises, you may be pleased to take notice, that no one stranger went with me but those French in the Ambassador's coach, which, without any least dispute whatsoever, did give place to my principal coach, as mine did to that which brought the Marquis, being the King's proper coach, a thing not formerly usual upon these occasions.—Ibid. p. 117.

SIR RICHARD FANSHAWE TO THE FRENCH AMBASSADOR.

I humbly thank your Excellency for the civility you showed to the King my Master, and the honour you did me, in sending your coach and domestics to accompany my entry;

and whereof I retain so lively a sense, that I am just going to acquaint my Master with it, not doubting in the least but it will meet with that esteem from him which your Excellency so highly deserves. My instructions, indeed, were to observe a more than ordinary intimacy and amity with your Excellency at this Court, which I shall always continue to do, and whereby I imagine we may not a little contribute towards the good and welfare of both kingdoms. I kiss your Excellency's hands, and wish you a long and prosperous life, being, My Lord,

Your Excellency's most obliged and most humble servant,

RICHARD FANSHAWE.—Ibid. p. 123.

To MR. SECRETARY BENNET.

Madrid, 2 July, 1664, Stilo Loci.

The herewith enclosed papers do contain my complaint of a studied neglect put by a Venetian Ambassador, whom I found in this Court ready to depart the same within a short time, upon the Ambassador of the King of England, in not giving me a visit either of welcome or farewell, as the custom of this and all other Courts do require in the like case; the which I have thought it my precise duty to represent to the King our Master, as knowing how highly the like neglect in the Court of England, by a Venetian Ambassador also, with others, towards an Ambassador, but of a Duke of Savoy, was resented; his then Majesty himself, in his Princely judgment, condemning the omission, as will here appear in the first place.

And lest this Venetian Ambassador should justify himself in this towards me, as pretending to be aggrieved by me, because I am entitled by his Catholic Majesty to the house of the Seven Chimeneas, which he was possessed of, and endeavoured to entail the same upon his successor, both against the decree of his Majesty and the consent of the owner, I having both, I do likewise herewith, in the following papers, make it clearly appear, that I did neither think of that individual house, till it was already embargoed for me, nor pursue it afterwards, as most men but myself would have done, being so destitute of conveniences of dwelling as I then was, and yet am, merely out of a respect I bear to the character of an Ambassador. So that, even in this particular, which is all the colour he can have for excuse of not visiting, I have just cause of a second complaint, but this second I totally let pass.

The other being much taken notice of by this Court as a matter of a more public nature, I humbly submit it to his Majesty's consideration, whether, in his Royal wisdom, he may not think fit to expostulate it with the Senate of Venice; in the mean time, his successor being arrived, I intend to send just such a message to him as his predecessor did to me; but have already declared, with the seeming approbation of all, that I will never give to, nor receive a visit from, this, or any Venetian Ambassador whatsoever, that shall be in this Court while I remain here, unless the King my Master, being applied to by the Republic, shall command it.—Ibid. p. 129.

To MR. SECRETARY BENNET.

Madrid, Thursday, 28th July, 1664, English Style.

You proceed expressing your gladness to hear I was housed in Madrid, upon which, after my humble thanks for the favour, I must needs observe the expression was very happy, if you rightly understand my case, and happier if you understand it not. Housed I have been here, that is, under a roof, these two months, making a shift with an upper quarter; such a one, indeed, as the Duke of St. German contained himself and family in; but a house I never had till this morning, then I had delivered into my possession the Casa de las siete Chimeneas.

This house was defended, for the space of time I have mentioned, against the King of Spain, and all his Aposentadores, [Footnote: Aposentadores are persons belonging to the Household, whose duties resemble those of the Harbingers in that of the Kings of England, namely, to provide lodgings on his journies or progresses. The office of Aposentador-Mayor is one of great honour and dignity.] by two Venetian Ambassadors successively; the first was really leaving it without any thought, as I am assured, of asking it for his successor; then the Duke of Medina de las Torres, when I never dreamed of it, and was in pursuit of another, procured it to be embargoed for me in reversion; this the Venetian apprehends an affront to him and his Republic; and whiles off the time of his stay here, to his great inconvenience, in respect of the advancing heats and otherwise, till he had got his successor up to him, marching furiously, who, contrary to the King and Council's expectation and express decree, doth amanecer in the Seven Chimeneas, fortifying himself there with his privilege of Ambassador, and makes it point of reputation so to do (patriacq. suacq.); in this security his predecessor leaves him about six weeks since, not to be removed with all the King and the Duke have been able to do, without imposition of hands, till the last night.

I dare confidently say nothing hath troubled both the Ambassadors so much in this whole business, as that they could never draw me in to make myself a party in the dispute; for as, at the first, I never asked that individual house; so when promised and decreed to me, I never insisted upon it, provided some other convenient one were found out for me, or that I myself could find out such a one for my money, and, effectually, about a fortnight since, did contract, under hand and seal, with the owner, for the entire house where I am, upon condition the Court did approve thereof; but the Duke told me, that must not be now, how well soever it might serve my turn, for the King would be obeyed in his own kingdom, and the Venetian should out. Upon the whole, all circumstances which I have seen, considered, it is to me apparent enough, that these Ambassadors of Venice, in this contest, did nourish double ambition, either to carry the house against an English Ambassador, or that an English Ambassador should carry it against them; but my business throughout hath been never to come in any competition or comparison with them.

This story I have been the longer in, because the matter thereof hath filled this Court, and may do some others, with as much noise, expectation, and, I do believe, secret sidings too, as it had been some very weighty interest of princes or states.

The heats of this summer have risen here proportionable to what you express of those in England.

"From a Letter to my Lord Holles, sent by mistake to my Lord Ambassador Fanshawe."

Whitehall, May 26, 1664.

"It is truly observed by you, that Monsieur de Lionne doth you wrong in not treating you with 'Excellency,' but then it is truly observed, that that style is quite out of use in that Court, and so much, that Frenchmen of any tolerable quality do not use it to their own Ambassador here, or in any other Court."—Ibid. p. 141.

To MR. SECRETARY BENNET.

Madrid, Wednesday, ..th July, 1664.

"Upon Sunday the 3d, stilo novo, of July, 1664, being the day of celebrating the Empress's birth, I attended his Majesty with the parabien; also, in the Queen's apartment, her Majesty, the Prince, and Empress: it was the first time I had seen the Prince."—Ibid. p. 142.

To MR. SECRETARY BENNET.

Madrid, Friday the 12th of August, 1664, N.S.

The design of the French courtesy in my public audience, even then perceivable and perceived, is now full blown; that the King hath in person expostulated with the Spanish Ambassador at Paris, why the King his Master would offer, by an innovation in the Spanish Court at that time, to bereave him, the said French King, of an opportunity of vindicating his just precedence of the King of England, and in pursuance thereof hath since sent letters to his Court to the same effect, and to demand restitution of the former custom in first entrances of Ambassadors from such others as they found here, which demand this French Ambassador hath done and doth manage to that degree of heat, with and in this Court, as, amongst other expressions, to have plainly threatened, that if he were not satisfied in this point, he would himself dispute the precedency with the Ambassador of the Emperor, I cannot say with the Pope's Nuncio too, because that hath not been told me, but the sequence is as if it had been so; for of certain, both the Emperor's Ambassador and Pope's Nuncio, and more, if not all, have addressed themselves to his Catholic Majesty, either by word of mouth or memorial, or both, (the which I do rather believe,) that since the French Ambassador did assume that liberty and privilege to himself, as to send his coach and family to the English Ambassador, contrary to the new order, it might be free for them to do the like to all other hereafter. All these particulars I have had from the Duke de Medina de las Torres; with this farther, that the French King enforced his said demand with many presents;

the Duke told me the matter is sub judice, and not determined; therefore, yesterday, having obtained audience, I presented to his Catholic Majesty, according to my late intimation to your Honour, the herewith enclosed protest, or not protest, as this or any other Court shall understand it, or rather as the King our Master, in his princely wisdom, shall interpret or command me to interpret the same, whose royal directions in the case, long since to be foreseen, I shall now by every post expect, for my better light, in case of revival of the former custom, which, by the packing of the cards, I conceive to be most probable; keeping myself in the interim that they come not upon my guard, the best I may.

The Venetian Ambassador's entry, which is next expected, can put me to no difficulty at all, in respect his predecessor never thought fit to give me a visit, either of welcome when I arrived, or farewell when he departed, whereof I formerly advertised you at large, and how such neglect hath been resented in another age. The Holland Ambassador, now resident mutato nomine, will have his entrada soon after; there will be some scruple, yet no very great one; on the contrary, I think there is a rational query whether I, or any other of the Ambassadors de Capilla [Footnote: Ambassadors of the first-class, who have the right to be covered at their audience of the Sovereign to whom they are accredited.] should visit him at all. The case is, in his quality of Resident he hath totally declined the visiting either the Emperor's, or me, or the French Ambassador; because the other two first, and then I, by their example, did not assent to treat him with 'Senoria Illustrissima,' and in our own houses with the hand and upper chair, this latter,

of giving him precedence in our own houses, being, I conceive, the only point he absolutely insists upon. Now if we do him wrong in this, why should we not right him whilst he is yet under the notion of Resident? And if we do him none, why should we visit the Holland Ambassador in our turn, when the Holland Resident, especially, being the same person, will not visit us in this?

Here is a Danish Resident, and an Enviado of Genoa, who stand off upon the very same terms both with those Ambassadors and with me. The latter having obliged me, by message, to solicit for the King our master's orders to guide me on behalf of his pretence, because I had sent him word, that without such I could not in discretion and civility, being a new comer, vary from the judgment and practice of my seniors in this Court.

Your Honour, by your long and late experience here, will understand the pinch of this business better than yet I do; who, by what I can learn, am of opinion, that according to the style of this Court, perhaps of all others likewise, a King's AMBASSADOR, in his own house, doth not give the hand to another King's RESIDENT, much less 'illustrissima,' twenty years ago; but then again, I am informed, that now these very Ambassadors of Germany and France, who may with justice enough make scruple of that, may at the same time give 'illustrissima,' and, within their own doors the hand, to a Ducal Ambassador, thereby preferring them to their own Residents: an old controversy not easily decided, and yet in a fair way to be so, when by strong inference we shall be found judges against ourselves. I have farther to avow, in justification of my not sending to accompany the Hollander in his entrada, or any other but a new French Ambassador, that having been myself accompanied from none of them who show themselves now so zealous to perform that function to others, I have no reason to perform it towards them, until I shall have received the King my master's particular direction therein, after knowledge of what hath passed.

This, by way of discussion, not of decision of the question; for although, by my seventeenth instruction, it is very clear I must give not the hand to any King's Ambassador, on which behalf his Majesty shall not need to doubt my zeal, neither, I hope, the success, how roughly soever the precedence may be jostled for, whether by them or theirs; yet, whether by receiving by such arts as are now on foot, and for such ends as are now declared, the forementioned custom of Ambassadors sending their coaches and families to each others entradas, be such a point of advantage above me, as in the same instruction I am commanded to be wary of; and whether, in that case, I am not to thrust in for a share, in as good a room as I can get by scratching for, since others by their unquietness, or by their inconstancy, impose the necessity, there will be the question; whereof I do now hope for resolution from his Majesty by every post, of what I formerly writ concerning this matter, then in prospect, and find, by your honour's last, that those despatches were at the writing thereof come newly to hand.—Ibid. p. 199.

TO MR. SECRETARY BENNET.

[See MEMOIRS, p. 179.]

Madrid, Wednesday, 12th of October, 1664, English style.

"Since my last to you of yesterday, the President of Castile having by the King's special and angry command, gone forth to the neighbouring villages, attended with the hangman, and whatsoever else of terror incident to his place and derogatory to his person, the markets in this town begin to be furnished again plentifully enough, yet so as that the bullion remaining fallen to the half value, bread, wine, and other provisions, are held up much higher than they were before in the numerical money; the reason is, whether upon intelligence or jealousy, the people that sell, do expect a second speedy fall, in which regard they rather choose to part with their wares upon trust, as many do and will, to receive for the same at the rate money shall go awhile hence, than for present money, though to persons whom before they would have been very scrupulous to have trusted."—Ibid. p. 265.

TO MR. SECRETARY BENNET.

[See MEMOIRS, p. 178.]

Madrid, Wednesday, 19th of October, 1664, English style.

Upon the 10th instant, stilo novo, invited by the delicacy of the weather, and not knowing whether I should have another opportunity for it during my residence in this Court, together with my family, man, woman, and child, I took a small journey by stealth, of three days going and coming, to Aranjuez.

As soon as it was known that I was gone, the Duke of Medina de las Torres sent a post after me, with a letter to myself, of courtly chiding, that I had given the Spanish civility the slip in that manner, with another to the officers of the palace, to perform their part towards me, which was not wanting in any needful degree, although the Propio [Footnote: The Duke's courier.] tracing me all the way, could not reach me till I got home again.

For the same reasons, we began another journey, upon Monday last, to the Escurial. [Footnote: Lady Fanshawe, p. 180, says they went to the Escurial on the 27th of October. Her Ladyship calculated by the NEW, and Sir Richard by the OLD style.] This was not, nor could be kept secret; therefore the Duke, prompting his Catholic Majesty, sent his orders before, by virtue whereof I was lodged in the quarter there of the Duke of Montaldo, Mayordomo Mayor to the Queen, and of like special order, by the Prior of that most famous monastery, showed, with all demonstrations of courtesy, the much that is there to be seen, besides an extraordinary present of provisions, of all which Don Juan Combos, whose company I was favoured with in this excursion, is able, if he pleases, to give you a better account than I.

Before I was returned half-way to this Court, we met some French, who told us the French Ambassador was following them to the Escurial. Advanced as far as a very small village, about a league from Madrid, the highway lying by a single house, at the outskirts thereof, at the door of the same, were two that wear his livery, of whom one of my people, asking whether the French Ambassador was coming towards the Escurial? they replied 'No;' but that his Excellency was in that village, and thence immediately to return to Madrid. That is all I yet know pertaining to that matter; unless this be, that it hath rained plentifully from morning to night, being, as the year hath fallen out, very extraordinary, the first day here of winter. Thus much may be built upon as a certainty, that neither the palace here upon Monday morning when I went, nor the Escurial this morning when I left it, had the least notice or inkling of any intention of the French Ambassador to go thither at this time.

A report there hath been for some days whispered, that the said Ambassador is revoken. To notify which the more, it is possible he might design this visit to the Escurial, which is commonly left to the last by all public persons from abroad.—Ibid. p. 267.

TO MR. SECRETARY BENNET.

Madrid, Wednesday, 12th November, 1664, N.S.

On Monday last, in the afternoon, I should by appointment have had a conference with the Duke of Medina de las Torres, but in the morning his Excellency sent to excuse it for that time, upon notice then arrived of the death of his kinsman, the Duke of Medina Sidonia, which obliged him to the offices which those cases require.

The manner of this Duke's death, like his quality, was extraordinary. His Excellency was, for his diversion and recreation, being as then in good health to all outward appearance, and not much stricken in years, at a town of his own, not far from Valladolid, where you know his constant appointed abode was; in that place of recreation, his Excellency had some number of dogs, newly given him, the which, looking out of his windows, he happened to see worrying a poor woman. They neither killed nor maimed her, but the Duke's apprehension was so great they would do the one or the other, that violently crying out from the place where he was unto his people to prevent it, he fell into a sudden cestacy; from that into a deep melancholy, and from that into a fever, which dispatched him before his physicians could come from Valladolid; so thereby verifying in his particular the surname of his family, de puro bueno murio.

Upon the 7th of November, N.S. I gave the King, Queen, Prince, and Empress, the parabien of the Prince's birth-day. The day itself was the precedent, and then it was that I desired audience to that end, by the Master of the Ceremonies; but it was appointed me, as I have said, to avoid concurrence with others, as I do believe, according either to the old or new style of this Court, the which I have formerly mentioned. However, for the English Ambassador alone, as might be supposed, all the royal persons put themselves de gala, both as to apparel and humour. True it is, to make up the jollity enough for two days at least, there met in one, and the parabien was accordingly both from the other Ambassadors the day before, and from me then, the Peace of Germany, and the Prince's birth-day, and both were very well taken.—Ibid. p. 290.

TO MR. SECRETARY BENNET.

Madrid, Monday, 14th of November, 1664, English style.

"Inclosed with this, I send you a print of that new invention here for ploughing, which you did lately command me to enquire out." [Footnote: Mr. Bennet, in a letter to Sir Richard Fanshawe, dated 29th of September, 1664, observed, "Sir George Downing tells me of a new invention of a plough in Spain. I beseech your Excellency to enquire after it. He saith an Italian hath made it, and that it is not only received in Spain, but sent into the Indies also, for the good of their land."—Ibid. p. 279.]—Ibid. p. 321.

TO MR. SECRETARY BENNET.

[See MEMOIRS, p. 185.]

Madrid, Wednesday, 14th of December, 1664, O.S.

These five or six nights last past here hath appeared a very strange blazing star, so high and so clear that I presume it must needs have been seen in England likewise, and therefore forbear to give any description or judgment thereof, the people of this country not being so curious in such matters as ours are there.

Yesterday I went to give the King and Queen the nova buena of her Majesty's birth-day, which was the day before. As soon as I came from the King, the Dutch Ambassador was called in; and at his coming out, it being a very dry day, and we having an hour to spend before the Queen would be ready to receive us, I invited him into my coach, and we took a turn in the town, which caused almost as much wonder in this people as the blazing star; and indeed I did it to that end partly, there being no offence in it that I know, so long as his Majesty hath an Envoy in Holland, and the States an Ambassador in England. The truth is, many of this people begin to apprehend, that our disputes with them will have a quite other issue, and a very different operation, as other interests, and Spain amongst the rest, than Spain imagined.

Last night was before the palace a masquerade on horseback. I had a balcony appointed me in the armoury over the stables of his Majesty: the Dutch Ambassador, another for him next below mine, the rest of the Ambassadors in an entresuelo of the palace.

Mine I left to my gentleman, and sat myself with the Duke of Medina de las Torres, at his quarters in the palace; my wife in another room thereby with the Duchess.—Ibid. p. 376.

TO THE LORD CHANCELLOR.

Madrid, the 24th of January, 1664, N.S.

MY LORD,

I send your Lordship herewith enclosed, two transcripts, the one of a project, at making of which I was never good; but this is of a peace, and therefore I wish I were; a peace between Castile and Portugal, hardly practicable upon any terms, as I do humbly conceive, much less upon these, proposed by an unknown author, with regard to either side; yet I have thought them not unworthy your Lordship's notice, as possibly more practicable elsewhere, as to form, and in a great measure as to matter likewise, than in the altitude for which they were designed.

The other transcript is of a fresh libel, in and upon this Court and palace; a commodity I have in my nature no inclination at all to vent, either by wholesale or retail; yet is this fit also, in my humble judgment, for persons of great nearness to his Majesty not to be unacquainted with, representing sores which are in foreign kingdoms, whereby to praise God the more for the modesty of ours at home, as ours for the great goodness of his Majesty that stops our mouths, or rather fills them with prayers to God and him; not censuring other princes, neither for the liberties of their subjects in their disparagement, much less these of Spain, than whom, from all times, none talk more against, or (our own nation only excepted) act more for, their kings. This damnable libel doth not spare one Councillor of State here present, but the Inquisidor General; and to crown the damnation of it, the King himself bears the burden, besides the smaller game it picks up by the way. So more than ordinary black is the Spanish ink at this day, and the mouths of two too many, loud ones too, much of the same dye.

This King, by what I can collect, as crazy as he is, may rub out many years: his Majesty eats and drinks ordinarily with a very good stomach, I am told, three comfortable meals a day; and full of merry discourse, when and where his lined robe of Spanish royal gravity is laid aside.

Some discourse begins to be of swearing the Prince. The sending the Infanta this spring to her Imperial Crown is absolutely concluded, say the most, and some say no. Certain it is, (the ceremony of this kingdom requiring it,) that a Cardinal in the spiritual, and some very great lay-person in the temporal, should be joint conductors of her Imperial Majesty; for the first, Cardinal Colonna, a vassal born of this Crown, chosen by the Pope, is now actually entered in this Court to the same end; and for the second, the Duke of Cardona, invited thereunto by his Catholic Majesty, after many great ones, namely, the Duke of Alva and Montaldo, had refused or excused it, hath publicly accepted the charge.

By this latter hangs a story. Your Lordship well knows, that in these more civilised countries, no man will go upon his master's errand without a reward beforehand, (so the Marquis of Sande, the Conde de Molina, and others innumerable,) therefore his Catholic Majesty, even after acceptance as a thing of course, was graciously pleased to bid the said Duke of Cardona propose for himself, referring him for that purpose to the Duke's friend, the Conde de Castrillo, President of Castile. The Duke tells the Conde he must have three things granted him in hand, else would he not budge a foot. 'What are those?' said the Conde, in some disorder. 'First,' said the Duke, 'I will be made a grandee of Spain,' and his Excellency is so, I take it three or four times over: 'Secondly, I will have the Toison' he has it long since: "Thirdly, the Conde de Chincon shall treat me with EXCELLENCY.' The riddle of this is, that the said Conde de Chincon, being no Grandee, and nominated for Ambassador Ordinary to the Emperor, though since excused of going for want of health, or other allegations, doth, upon that account alone, during life, according to the style of this Court, remain with the title of Excellency. This action of the Duke of Cardona is here very much celebrated, and the saying little less. —Ibid. p. 420.

To THE KING.
[See MEMOIRS, p. 195.]
Madrid, Monday, 6th of February, 1664-5, O.S.
"MAY IT PLEASE YOUR MAJESTY,

"The bearer hereof, Mr. Charles Bertie, son to the Earl of Lindsey, having done me the honour, together with other gentlemen of rank and personal worth, to afford me his company out of England hitherto, and now with them homewards bound by the way of France; I find myself encouraged by the opportunity of so noble a hand for conveyance, to give your Majesty this first immediate trouble of any lines of mine, since I had last the happiness to kiss that of your Majesty, as well to throw myself, in all humility, at your royal feet, as to render very briefly a faithful character of this young gentleman, in a more particular manner, whose virtues and extraordinary qualities, the former not lost, the latter acquired with much travels at few years, do no whit degenerate from the nobility of his blood, and active loyalty of his progenitors; my duty to your Majesty, as well as my affection to his person, obliging me ex officio to this short testimony of his merits unrequested, to the end so hopeful a branch of that house may not want even this means among others, of being early known to his Sovereign, I could humbly wish I could add, his master too, and that in some near degree of service to your sacred person, for the present, in order to public employment for the future; towards which, as years shall increase, and occasions be ministered, he is already furnished, in a very good measure, with two principal and proper gifts, that of tongues, and that of observation. But I forget to whom I speak, for which most humbly begging your royal pardon, I crave leave to subscribe myself," &c.—Ibid, p. 437.

To MR. SECRETARY BENNET.
Madrid, Tuesday, 18/28 April, 1665.

This King, with the Queen and Empress, have now been almost a fortnight at Aranjuez, to their great content, and also of this Court, to hear his Majesty is so vigorous there, as at one time to have set on horseback a matter of three hours, and in that posture to have killed a wolf from his own hands; whereas, before his going hence, it was doubted by many whether he had sufficient health and strength to perform the journey, though but seven leagues, in a coach or litter, and that in two days. The little Prince remains here in the palace, as far as I can learn, nothing so lively as his father; pray God he prove so lasting!

In this interim, Don John de Austria hath had leave to reside at a house within two leagues of Aranjuez, and from thence stepping over to get a sight of his Majesty, which he did. The ceremony between them was very short, and yet all that passed was ceremony; Como venis? Como estays? Dios os guarde, &c., with which his Highness departed to the Queen and Empress, and from thence to whence he came, after the same brief ceremony; only the Queen and Empress sent him each of them a jewel for a present.—Harleian MSS. 7010, f. 239.

TO LORD ARLINGTON.
[See MEMOIRS, p. 200.]
Madrid, Wednesday, August 1665.

My last to your Lordship of this day was a se'nnight, made mention of a conference I was to have the Friday following with the Duke of Medina de las Torres, but it happened the same Wednesday night I fell so extremely sick as forced me on Thursday to send my excuse to his Excellency, continuing my bed all that day, and since my house, though, I thank God, with some amendment daily, and now to such a competent degree of health and strength, that upon Friday next I hope our meeting will hold.

In the mean time, upon occasion of my wife's being brought to bed, on Sunday, the Duke hath been with me to give me the joy of my son, yet so as not to mingle therewith one word of business, making that expressly a piece of the compliment; the rest consisting of great riches of jewels upon his person, and extraordinary splendour of equipage.—Ibid. f. 346.

TO LORD ARLINGTON.
[See MEMOIRS, p, 201.]
Madrid, Thursday, 7/17th September, 1665.

My letter to your Lordship, delivered his Catholic Majesty, King Philip the Fourth, in a condition utterly deplored by most, though with a little spark of hope in some, even physicians, upon a lightening that showed itself before death as it proved, his Majesty giving up the ghost this morning between four and five of the clock, witnessed immediately by all the bells in the town; this being somewhat observable in my opinion, that neither his Majesty's sickness, nor his death, was concealed one moment from the people. Some care is taken that the news thereof shall not be sent out of these kingdoms till it hath first gone by their own Correos, stopping all others.

In observation of the custom which ought to be observed in like cases, the Council of the Chamber of Castile met to open his Majesty's testament, which he left closed; the which accordingly was opened and read before the President and said Council, by Don Blasco de Loyola, Secretary of the Universal Dispatch: this was done at eleven of the clock this forenoon. His Majesty left the Queen declared Governess of his kingdoms, assisted by four counsellors ex-officio, viz., the Archbishop of Toledo, that is or shall be; the President of Castile, that is or shall be; the Vice-Chancellor of Arragon, that is or shall be; the management of the kingdom, in like cases, belonging, by ancient laws of the kingdom, to these three dignities, though his Majesty should omit to name them; and the Inquisitor-General, that is or shall be: he is introduced by a new law. His Majesty added to this number of four, two more, one for a Grandee of Spain, which is the Marquis of Aytona; and the other, who is the Conde de Penaranda, for Counsellor of State. His Majesty left for executors of this his will, the Duke of Medina de las Torres, Fray Juan Martinez, who was his Majesty's confessor, and the Marquis de Velada.

Don John of Austria came post from Consuegra, soliciting to see his Majesty by the means of the President of Castile, who, telling his Majesty that Don John desired his blessing, his Majesty answered, 'He had not called him, and that he should return presently;' which he did, as soon as the King expired. This as to the seeing him at the King's hour of death; but for all that, it is said, his Majesty had already so far remembered him in his will as to recommend therein to the Queen and her assistants, his son Don John of Austria, to regard him and employ him, and if the means he hath be not found sufficient for his support, to augment the same in some other way. [Footnote: In the margin, Sir Richard has written, "Sic transit gloria mundi."]

It is said it will not be necessary to make more ceremony for the giving of obedience to the new King Charles the Second, than with a banner upon the tower of St. Salvador, to proclaim, 'Castilla, Castilla por el Rey Don Carlos Segondo nuestro Senor!' and this ought to be done by the Conde de Chinchon, unto whom, being Regidor of Madrid, it belongs to execute the said ceremony.

They have embalmed his Majesty, and found in one of his kidneys a stone of the bigness of a chestnut, in the other a kind of thin web. They put his dead body, open-faced, with the state accustomed, in the great gilded hall of the Palace; and upon Saturday, at night, will carry it to the Escurial to be interred in the incomparable Pantheon there, begun by his grandfather, carried on by his father, and finished by himself in his life-time to a ninth wonder, if the Escurial be the eighth, as the Spaniards term it.—Ibid. f. 387.

TO LORD ARLINGTON
Madrid, Wednesday, 18/28 October, 1665.

"This evening I have had audience of the young King; giving him, in our Master's name, first the pesame, and then the parabien of the time. On Friday, begin the honras of the King, his father; after which, and, as I do believe, on the 5th of the next month, because it is the King's birth-day, the Queen will give her first audience to Ambassadors; none having yet seen her Majesty but the German, and he in his private capacity."—Ibid. f. 415.

FROM LORD SANDWICH TO SIR RICHARD FANSHAWE
[See MEMOIRS, p. 211]
La Coruna, March 20/30, 1666.

MY LORD,
Being arrived at this place through necessity of the weather, which put us off from Santander, whither we were designed, I find it requisite to give speedy notice thereof to Madrid, and in the first place to your Excellency; hoping this letter will have the good fortune to meet you there, and if it do, I then beseech you, either from yourself to give notice to the Court of my arrival, or direct this gentleman, Mr. Weeden, of whom I have great esteem, to deliver the letter he hath from me to the Secretary of State, a copy whereof is here enclosed, if your Excellency doth not think fit that the same be signified to the Court both ways. I also farther entreat your favour in sending me such advice for my journey, and procuring me such helps and furtherances therein, as may enable me to accomplish it with most expedition. Mr. Weeden is fully instructed in the condition of my retinue and carriage; and as the affairs of both Crowns, the time of the year, and other circumstances considered, require much haste to be made in this negotiation, so the particular interest of the King our Master, needs as speedy a meeting as can be between your Excellency and me, which I pray

to have in your mind, and contrive in the best manner you can. In the meantime, as soon as anything is concluded by you fit for my notice, I pray you to despatch Mr. Weeden back to me, whether I remain in this place, or shall be on my way to Madrid. I have not more to say unto you fit for a letter, but to desire you to present my most humble service to my noble Lady, and that you would believe that I come with that respect and resolution of doing you a service, and of expressing myself upon all occasions,

My Lord,

Your Excellency's most humble servant,

SANDWICH.-Ibid.

To LORD SANDWICH.

Madrid, April 1/11, 1666.

"My wife returns many humble services to your Excellency, hoping my good Lady's health; and likewise to be sooner happy in waiting upon her than your Excellency, as, taking her leave this very day hereof of the Queen and Empress, bound for England, at her good old father's long importunities, to have his dear daughter and all her children rest with him before he dies."—Ibid.

FROM LORD SANDWICH to SIR RICHARD FANSHAWE. (ORIGINAL.)

From My Quinta, near the Corunna, April 9/19, 1666.

"It is my great misfortune that I am like to miss of the happiness of kissing my good lady's hand at Madrid, to whom my wife and I are so infinitely obliged. The best satisfaction I can have next, is to hear that her ladyship hath good health and prosperity on her journey; which I most heartily wish, as I do all sorts of occasions, whereby to express unto her ladyship and yourself with what fidelity, I am,

My Lord,

Your Excellency's most humble and most obedient Servant,

SANDWICH.—Ibid.

TO THE LORD CHANCELLOR.

Madrid, Thursday, 15/29 April, 1666.

"The Empress, married by proxy, which was the Duke de Medina de las Torres, upon Sunday last, did yesterday begin her journey from this Court towards Vienna. Her Imperial Majesty carried along with her a vast treasure in money, plate, and jewels; so, in that respect, will much enfeeble this summer's preparation against Portugal: in another regard the despatch of that great affair out of the way, which hath wholly taken up these Councils in pro's and con's for many months past, hath left them at liberty to prosecute with the more vigour this war."—Ibid.

TO SIR PHILIP WARWICK.

Madrid, 3rd of May, 1666, s n.

DEAR BROTHER,

There was due to me on 6th of March last past, upon my ordinary entertainment, the sum of two thousand pounds, of which I have not yet received one shilling, notwithstanding that I was forced to run myself in debt for my late journey to Portugal; as I have written long since to my Lord Arlington, requesting I might, by his Lordship's means, obtain a particular Privy Seal for the reimbursement of my laying-out therein, as was promised when that case should arrive.

Moreover, I have both pawned and sold plate for my present subsistence, and if immediately I do not receive a supply of all that is due to me upon amount of ordinaries, the which I do hopefully expect upon former addresses to that purpose, I cannot subsist longer in this Court, nor yet know how to remove out of it, if such should be his Majesty's orders of revocation, by my Lord of Sandwich: a thing intimated to me here by more than common persons, whether with or without ground I cannot say, having not heard one word from any Minister of our Court for the space of above seven weeks last past, or concerning myself anything out of England, save what I read in a London diurnal, that letters from me out of Portugal, by sea, signifying my then immediate return for Madrid, were come to hand. The like whereof having never happened to me before, so much as for a fortnight's time, I am utterly to seek what to impute it to, unless it be interceptings in France since the war hath been declared. In the meantime, it puts me to a great confusion in many respects, particularly for the want of monies; and thus farther I crave leave to inform you upon the same point, which is, that if my brother Turnor's kindness had not advanced out of his own purse, to comply with my bills, above a thousand pounds, before he received the last tallies on my behalf, whereof I have not had any notice, I had been reduced to yet greater extremities than these I am contending with.

Having thus delivered the truth of my condition in matter of fact, I presume there will need nothing farther of argument, with so good a friend and brother, to quicken and keep alive your constant endeavours for me, or indeed with such others whose concurrence is necessary to render your brotherly offices effectual, to afford the same accordingly, upon the mere account of our Master's honour and service, without other relation to the person that bears his image in this particular.

I pray you, as you have done hitherto, permit my brother Turnor to remind you of these things as often as occasion shall require.

My Lord Sandwich, according to our computation here, will begin his journey towards us to-morrow from the Corunna, and if his Excellency makes no stop by the way will arrive in this Court about twenty days hence, hardly sooner. I rest, dear brother, your most affectionate brother and faithful servant,

RICHARD FANSHAWE.—Ibid.

TO HIS MAJESTY.

Madrid, Thursday, 3rd of June, 1666, stilo loci.

MAY IT PLEASE YOUR MOST EXCELLENT MAJESTY,

By the hands of my Lord of Sandwich, who arrived in this Court, upon Friday last, was delivered to me a letter of Revocation from your Majesty, directed to the Queen Regent; and at the same time another, with which your Majesty honoured me for myself, implying the principal, if not the only, motive of the former to have been, some exceptions that had been made to the papers which I signed with the Duke of Medina de las Torres, upon the 17th of December last past;[Footnote: Sir Richard Fanshawe wrote in the margin of the rough transcript, "Relating to the Commerce of this Crown, and the establishing a Truce between these and Portugal."] a consideration sufficient to have utterly cast down a soul less sensible than hath ever been mine of your Majesty's least show of displeasure, though not accompanied with other punishments, if your Majesty, according to the accustomed tenderness of your royal disposition, in which you excel all monarchs living, to comfort an old servant to your Majesty, had not yourself broken the blow in the descent, by this gracious expression in the same letter: That I may assure myself, your Majesty believes I proceeded in the articles signed by me, as aforesaid, with integrity and regard to your royal service, and that I may be farther assured the same will justify me towards your Majesty, whatever exceptions may have been made to my papers.

In obedience to your Majesty's letter above-mentioned, I make account, God willing, to be upon my way towards England some time next month; having in the interim performed to my Lord Sandwich, as I hope I shall to full satisfaction, those offices which your Majesty commands me in the same; whose royal person, council, and undertakings, God Almighty preserve and prosper many years; the daily fervent prayer of

Your Majesty's ever loyal subject, ever faithful and most obedient servant,

RICHARD FANSHAWE.

FROM LYONEL FANSHAWE, ESQ., TO JOSEPH WILLIAMSON, ESQ.

[See MEMOIRS, p. 217.]

Madrid, Thursday, 7/17 June, 1666.

My Lord having been taken with a very sharp fit of sickness two days since, and not yet being well able either to write or dictate a letter himself, hath commanded me to entreat you, that you will please to present his most humble service to my Lord Arlington, and beseech his Lordship to excuse his not writing by this post.

The Empress is said not to be yet embarked, though there are thirty galleys ready to attend her in her voyage.

My Lord of Sandwich hath not, as yet, had his first public audience. Sir Robert Southwell intends, within a day or two, to begin his journey for Portugal.—Ibid.

THE FORM OF A PRAYER USED BY MY LORD'S CHAPLAIN, IN THE DAILY SERVICE IN HIS EXCELLENCY'S CHAPELIN PORTUGAL AND SPAIN.

Blessed God, we beseech thee to be propitious in a singular manner to my good Lord, his Excellency, his Majesty's Ambassador in this kingdom; preserve him unto us in health and strength, and grant that he may so manage those weighty affairs he is employed in, that the issue of his negotiation may be to thy glory, the satisfaction of our Sovereign, and the mutual good and benefit of all his subjects and allies. Bless his most virtuous Lady; imbue her with the blessings of this life, and that to come; make his children thy children, his servants thy servants, that this family may be a Bethel, a house of God; that we, all serving thee with one accord here on earth, may for ever glorify thee in Heaven. Amen.

A PRAYER USED IN THE DAILY SERVICE OF THE CHAPEL, AFTER THE DEATH OF HIS EXCELLENCY THE LORD AMBASSADOR.

Blessed God, which suppliest the wants and relievest the troubles of thy servants, be particularly gracious to this family, and here, in a special manner, bless my most virtuous Lady, and give her patience under thy hand, submitting to thy will, and contentedness under every change; and we beseech thee so continually to assist her in the course of her life, that she may experimentally find thee a God all- sufficient, though the helps of this world fail: make her children thy children; bestow upon them thy choicest blessings, who hath promised to be a father to the children's children of those that trust in thee; make her servants thy servants, that this family may be a Bethel, a house of God; that we, all serving thee with one accord here on earth, may for ever hereafter glorify thee in Heaven. Amen.

CPSIA information can be obtained at www.ICGtesting.com
Printed in the USA
BVOW04s2355200115

384235BV00016B/207/P